Swear Word Coloring Book

A Swearing Coloring Book for Adults containing over 40 Sweary, Funny and Abusive Pattern Designs

by The Coloring Book People

ISBN-13: 978-1523777549

ISBN-10: 1523777540

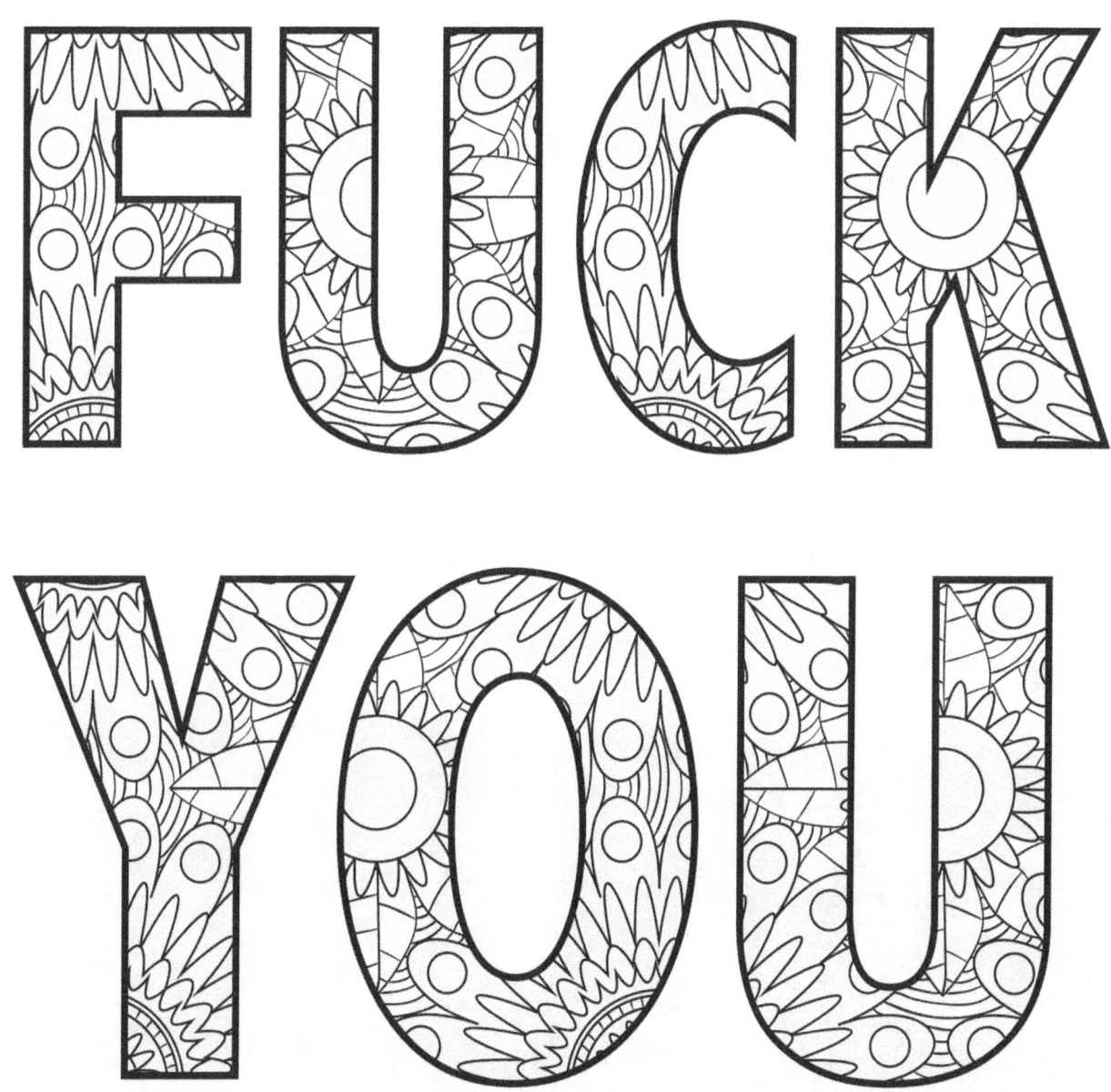

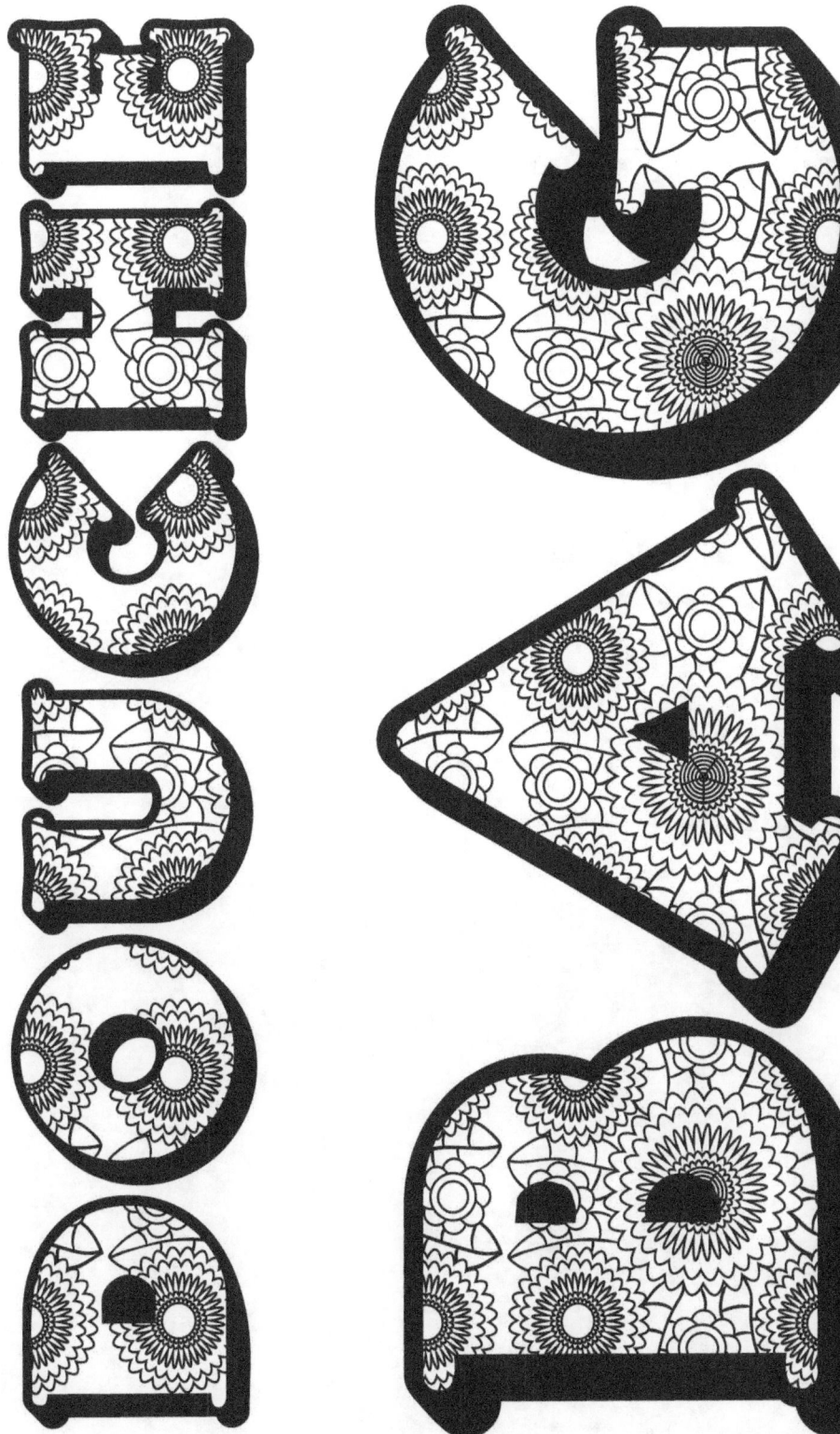

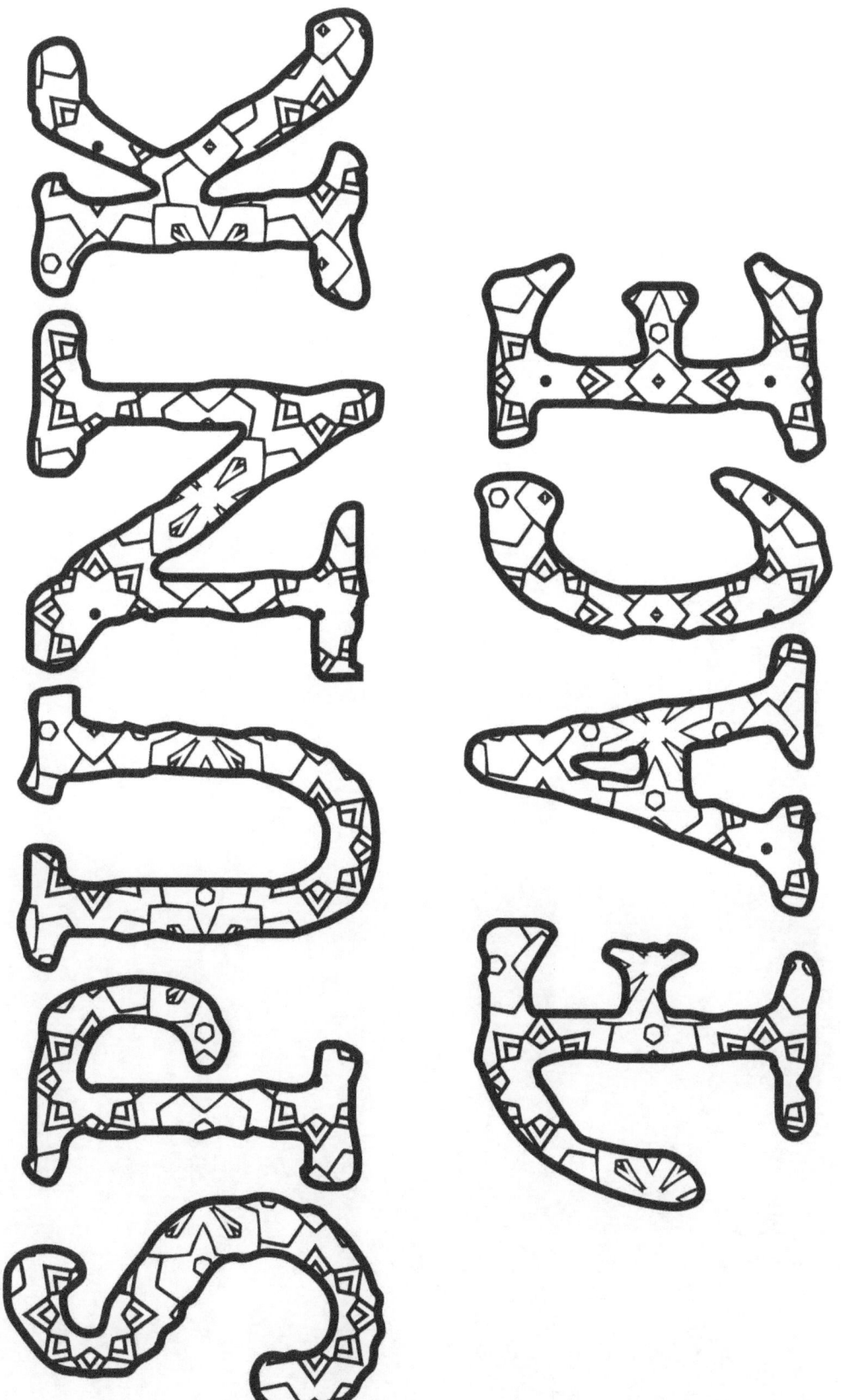

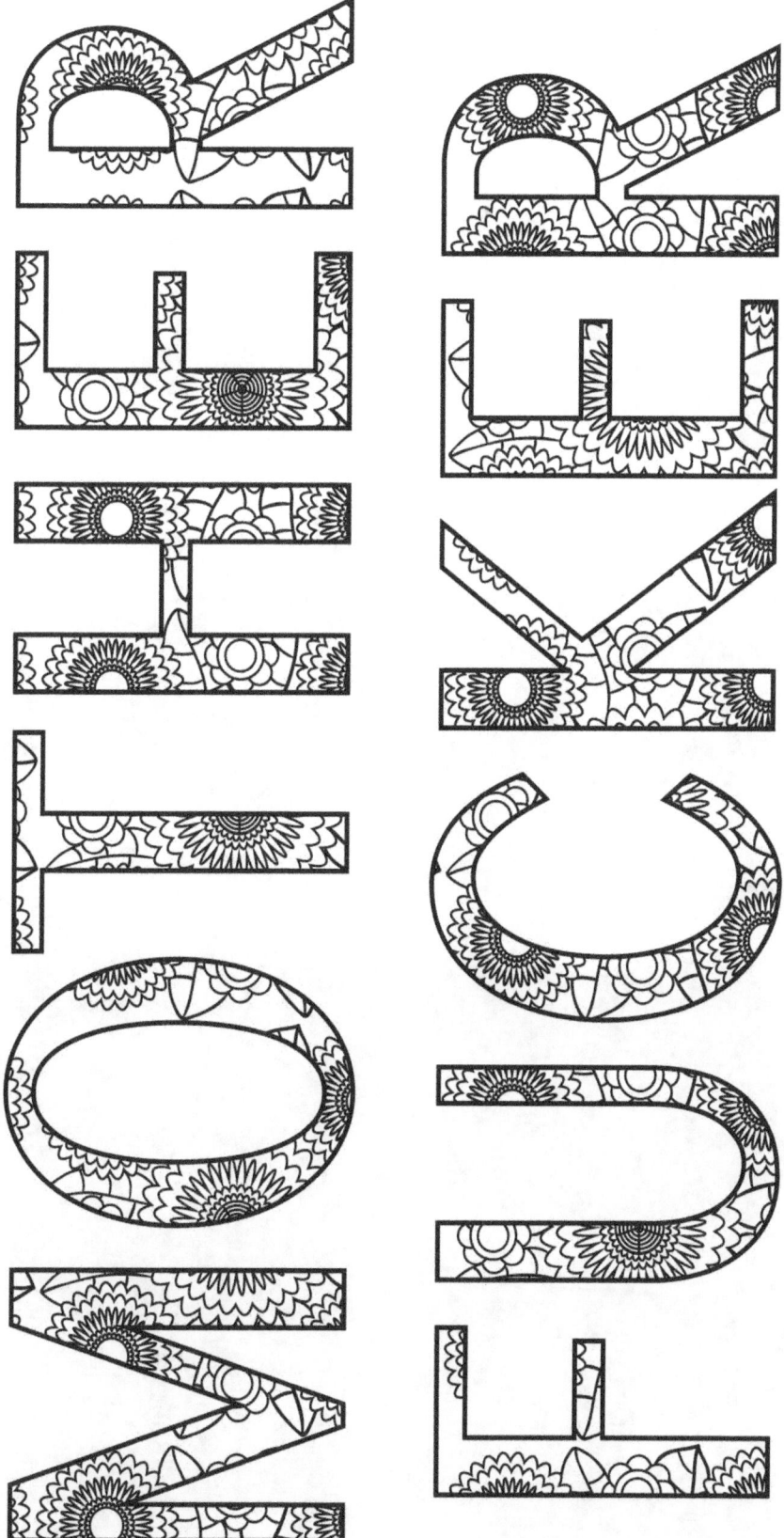

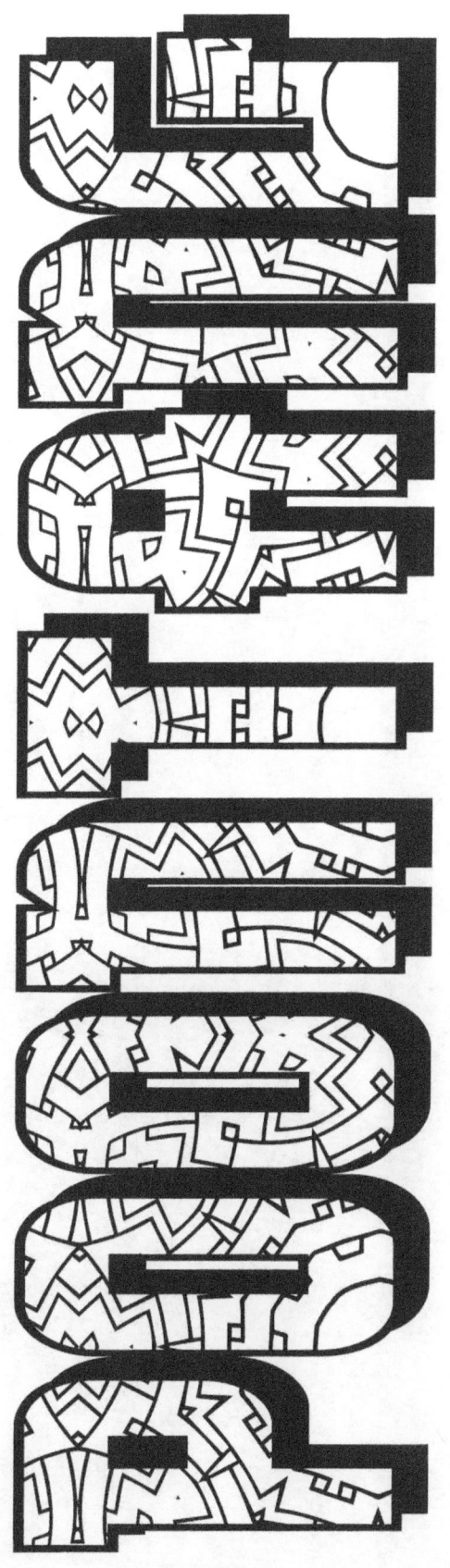

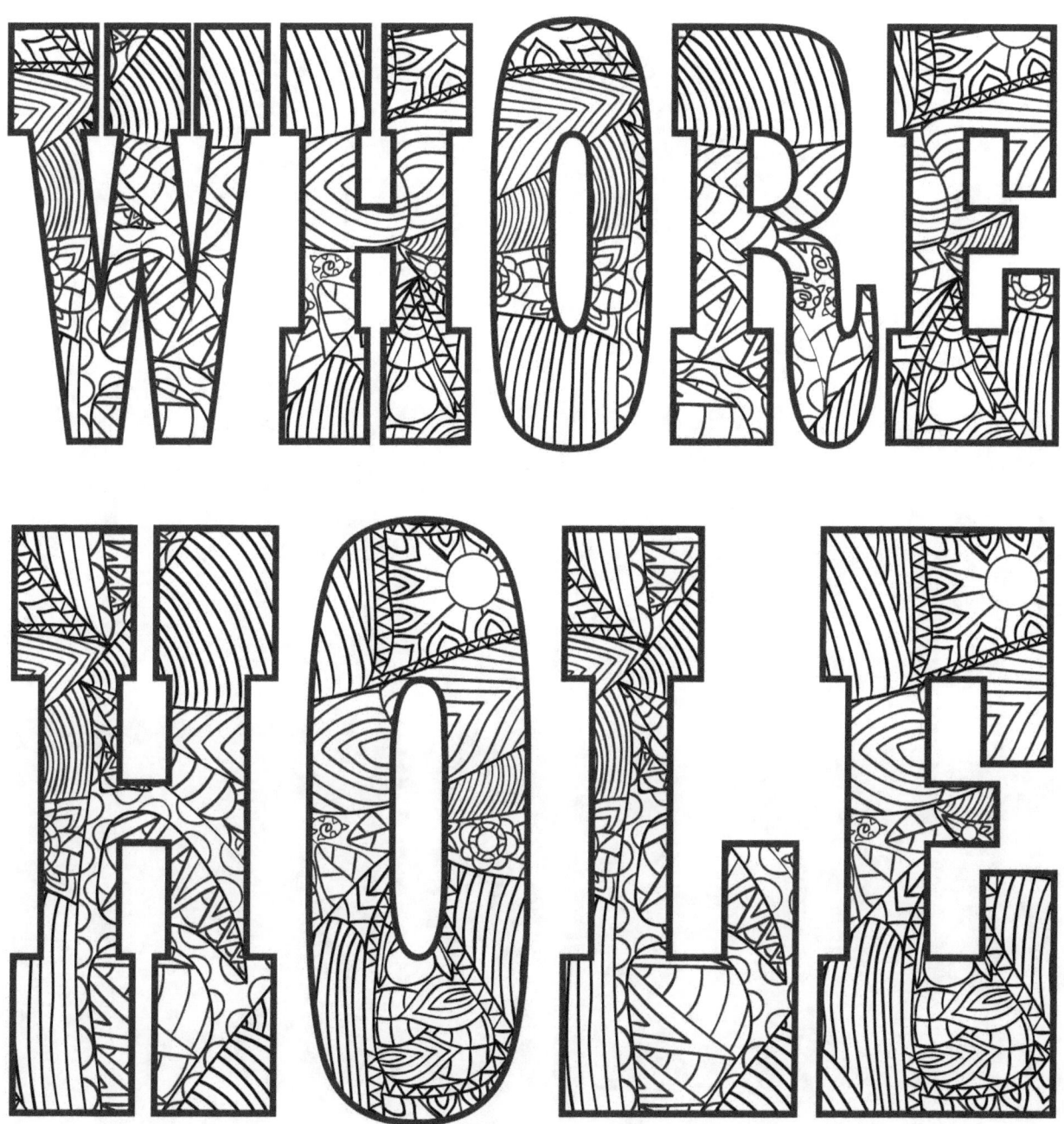

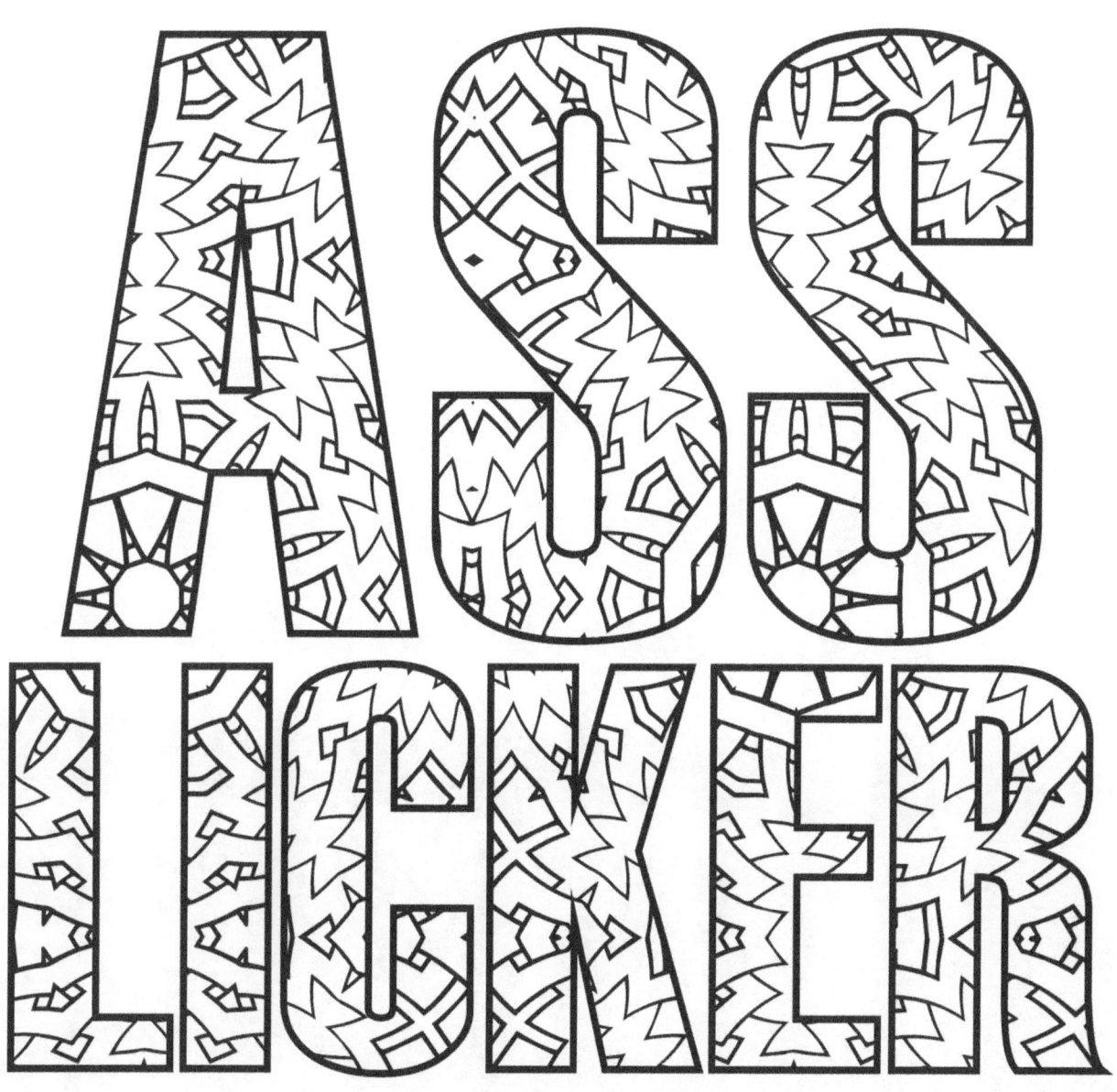

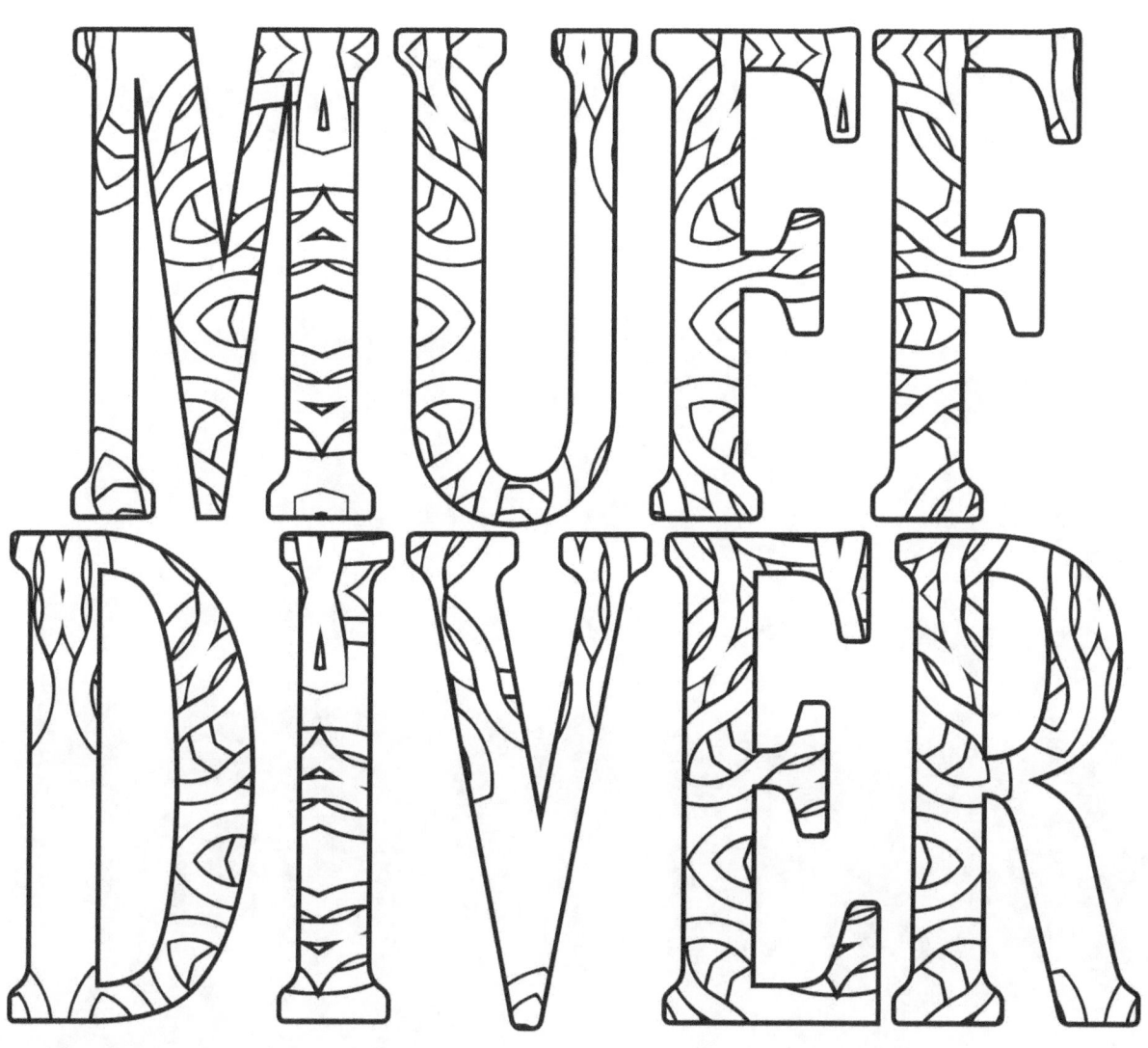

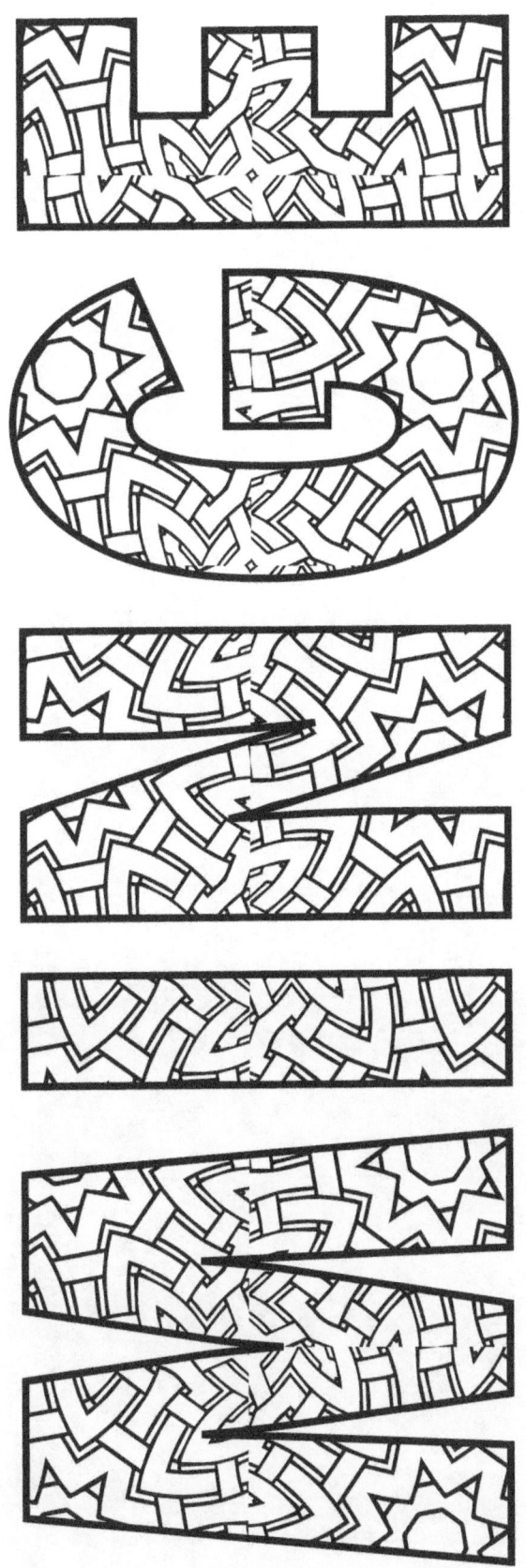

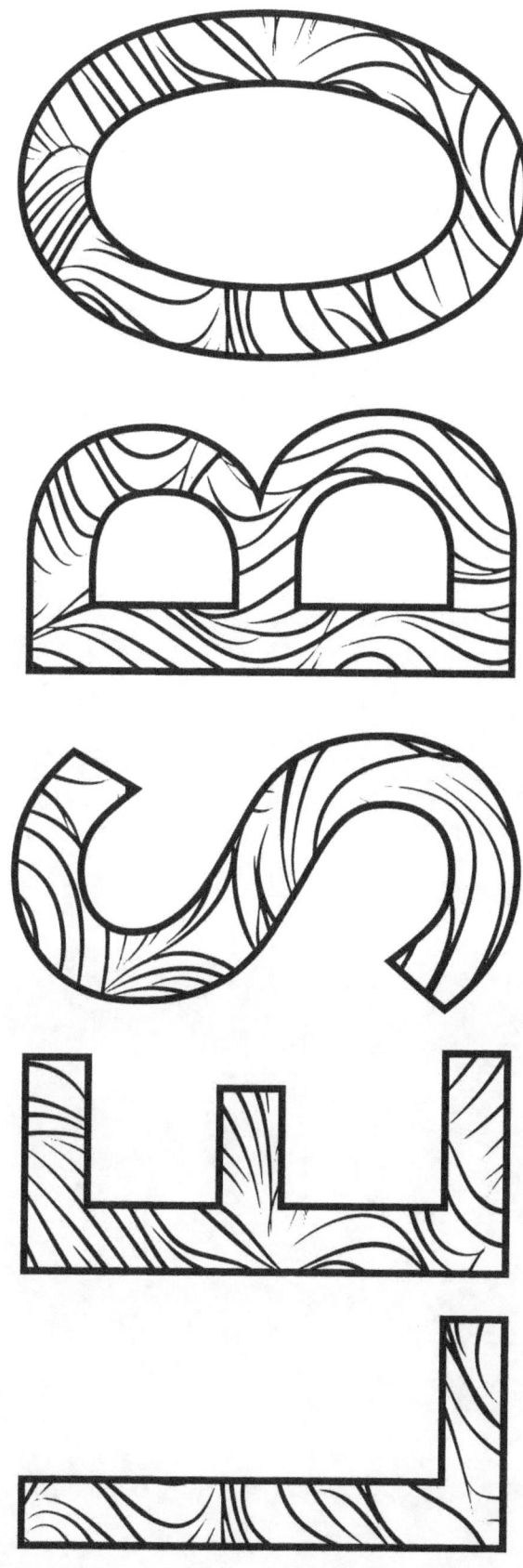

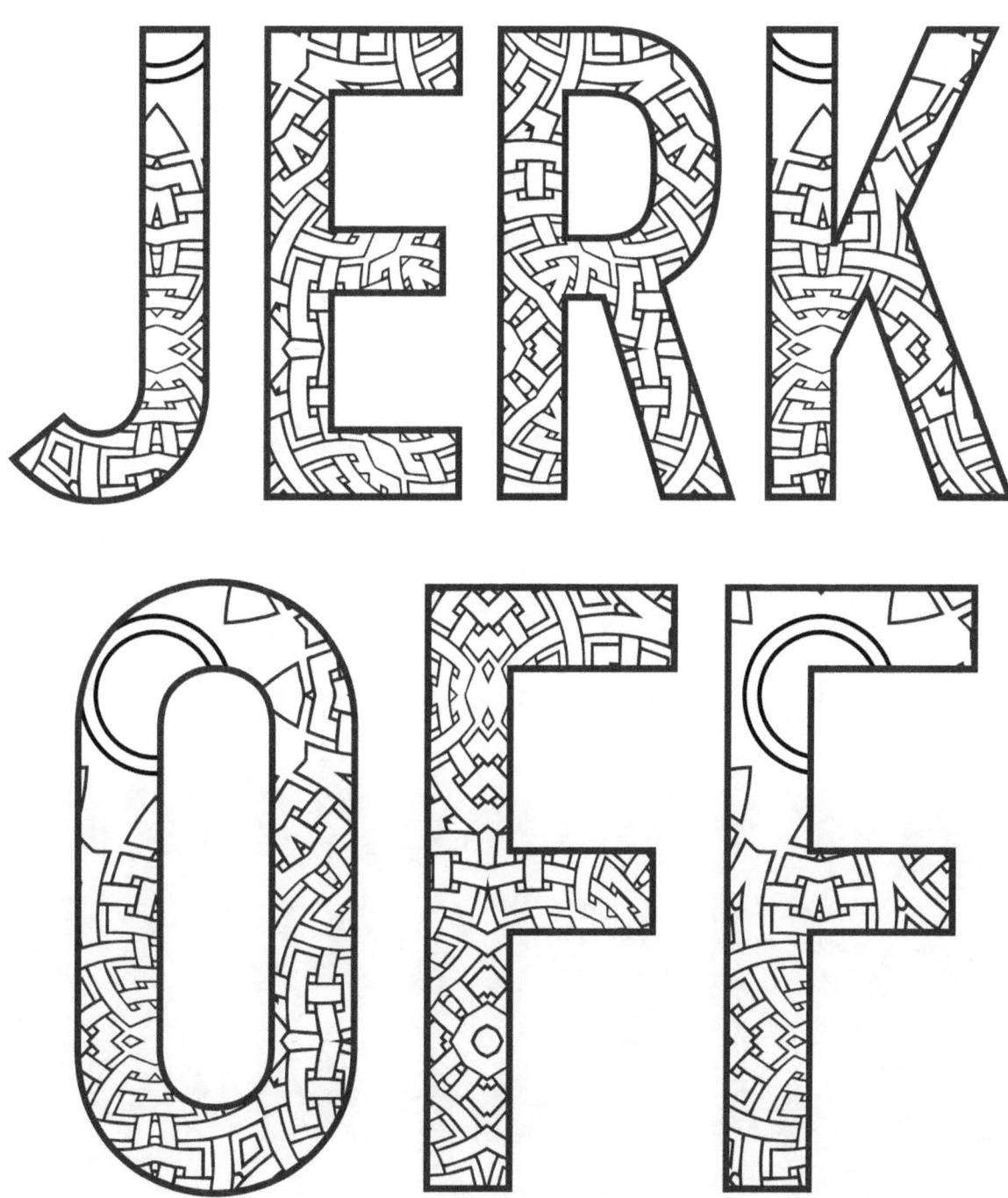

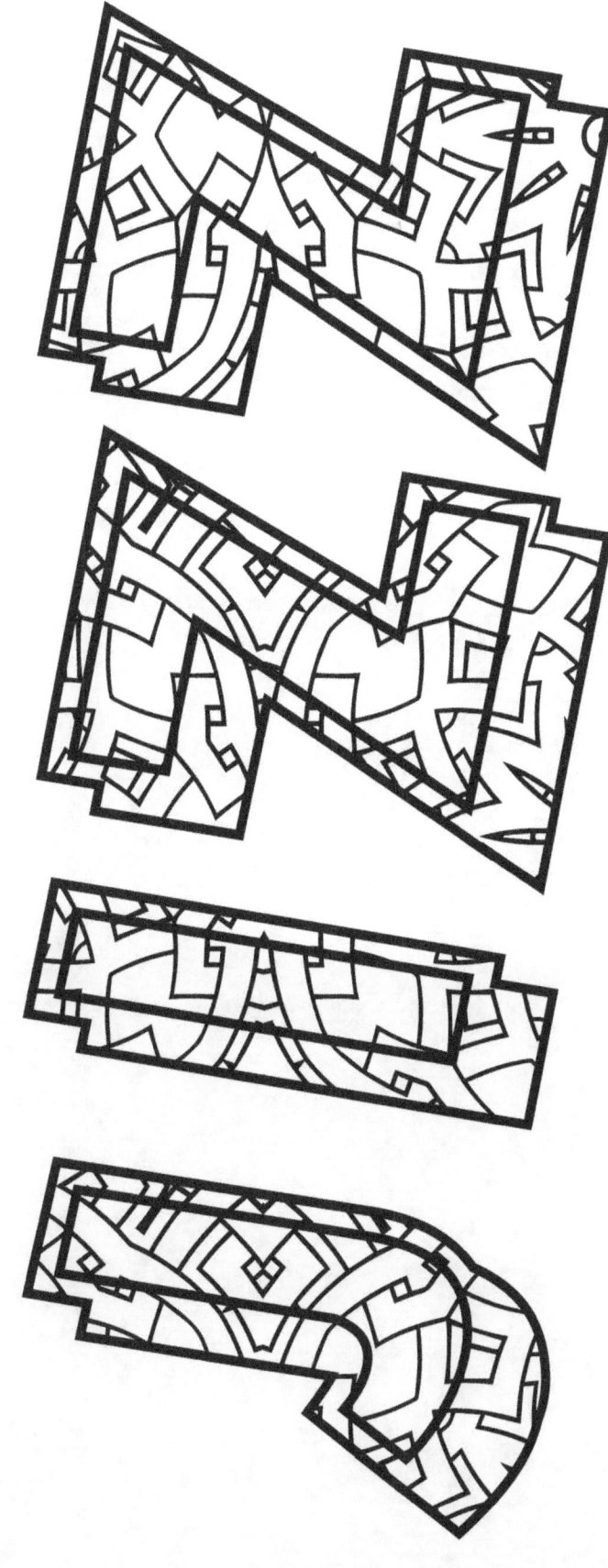

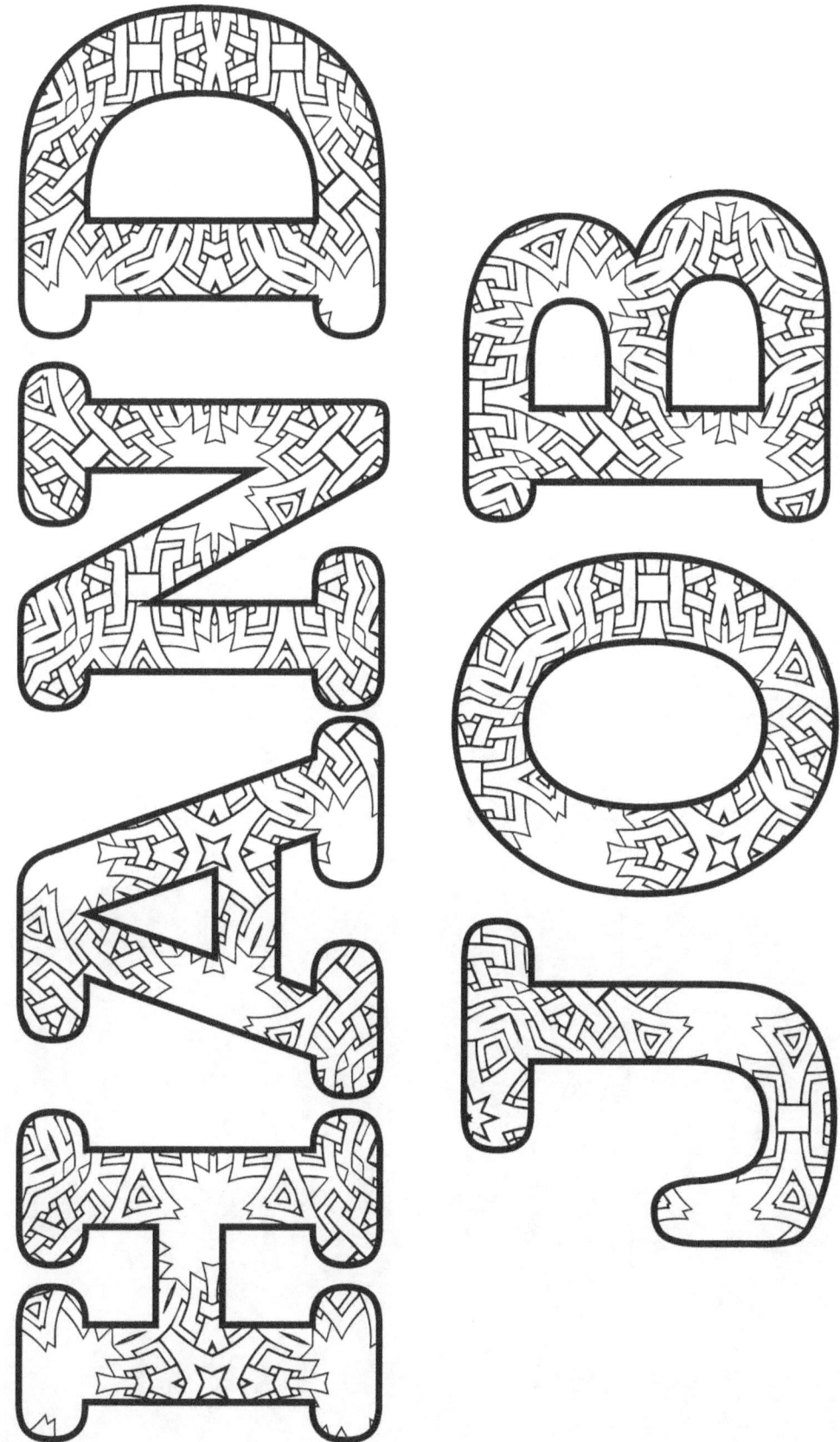

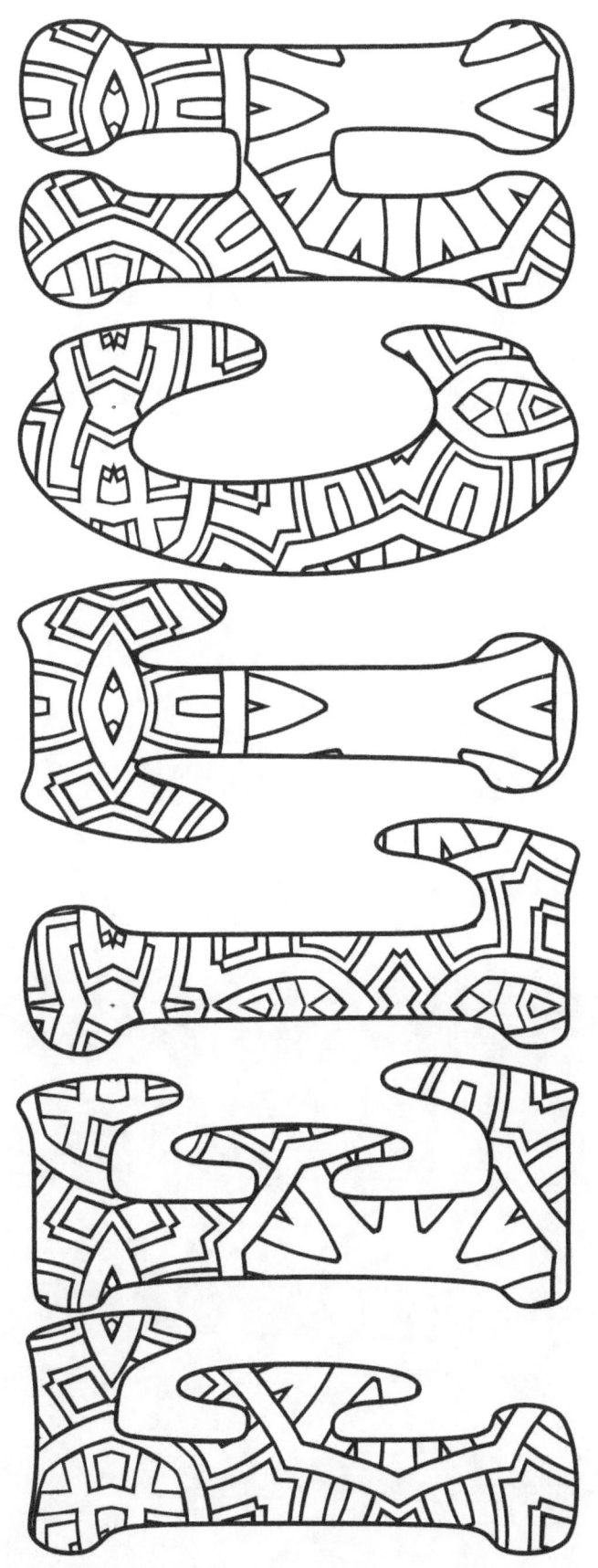

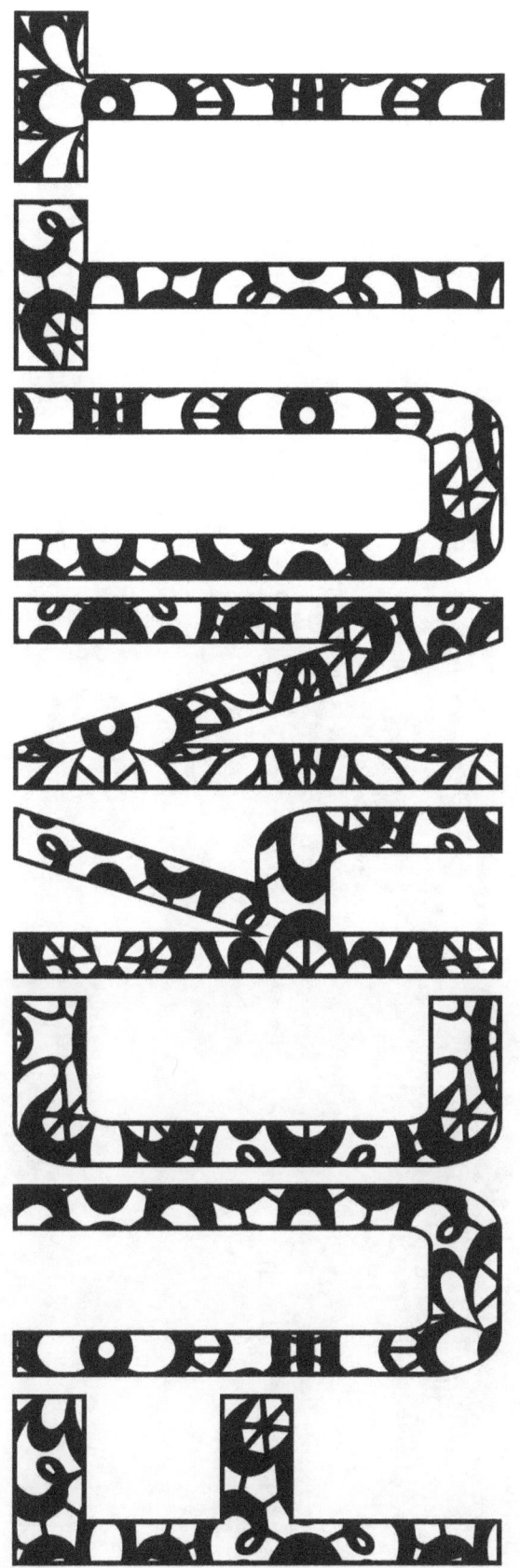

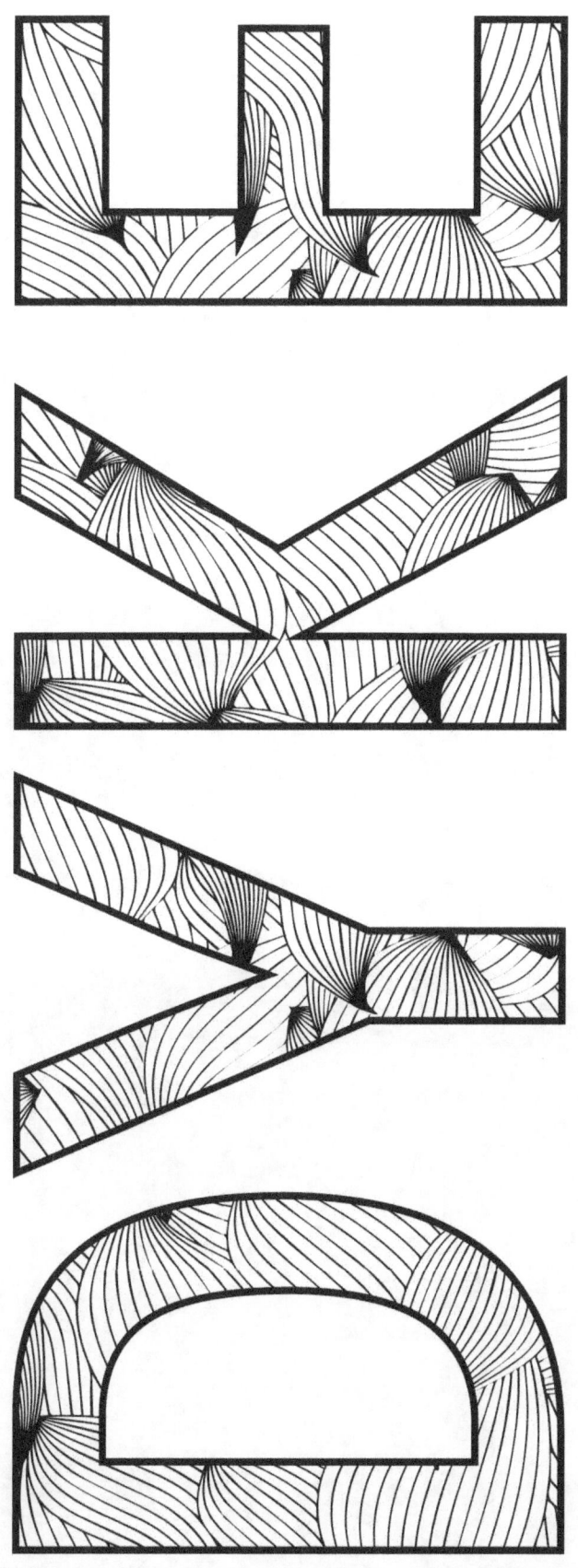

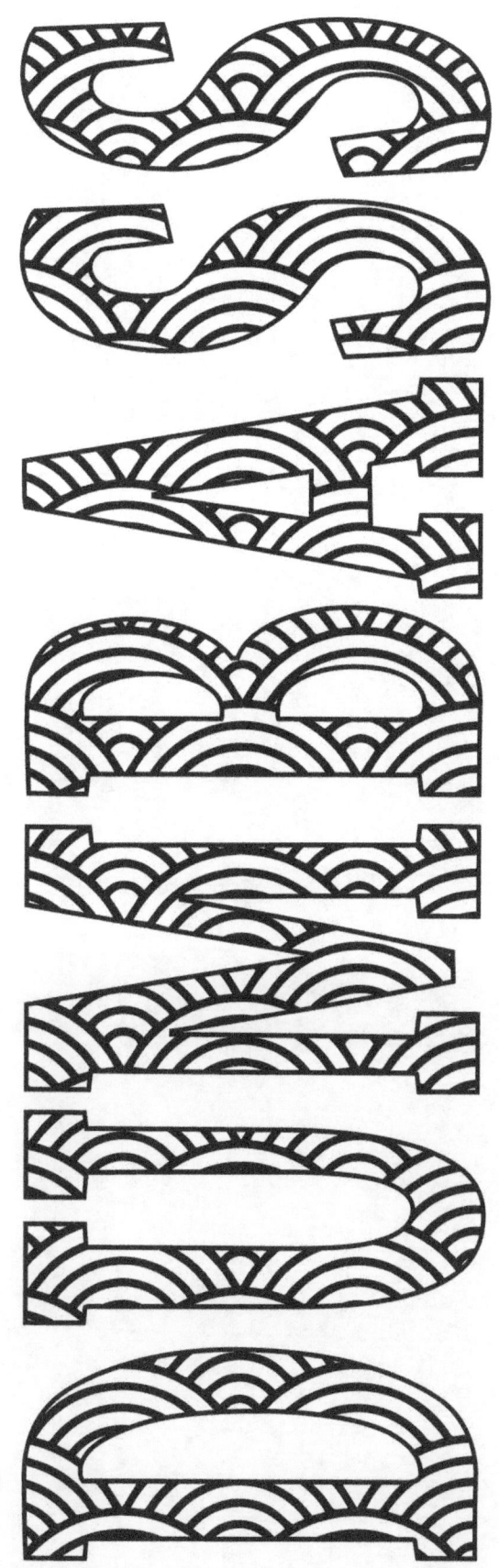

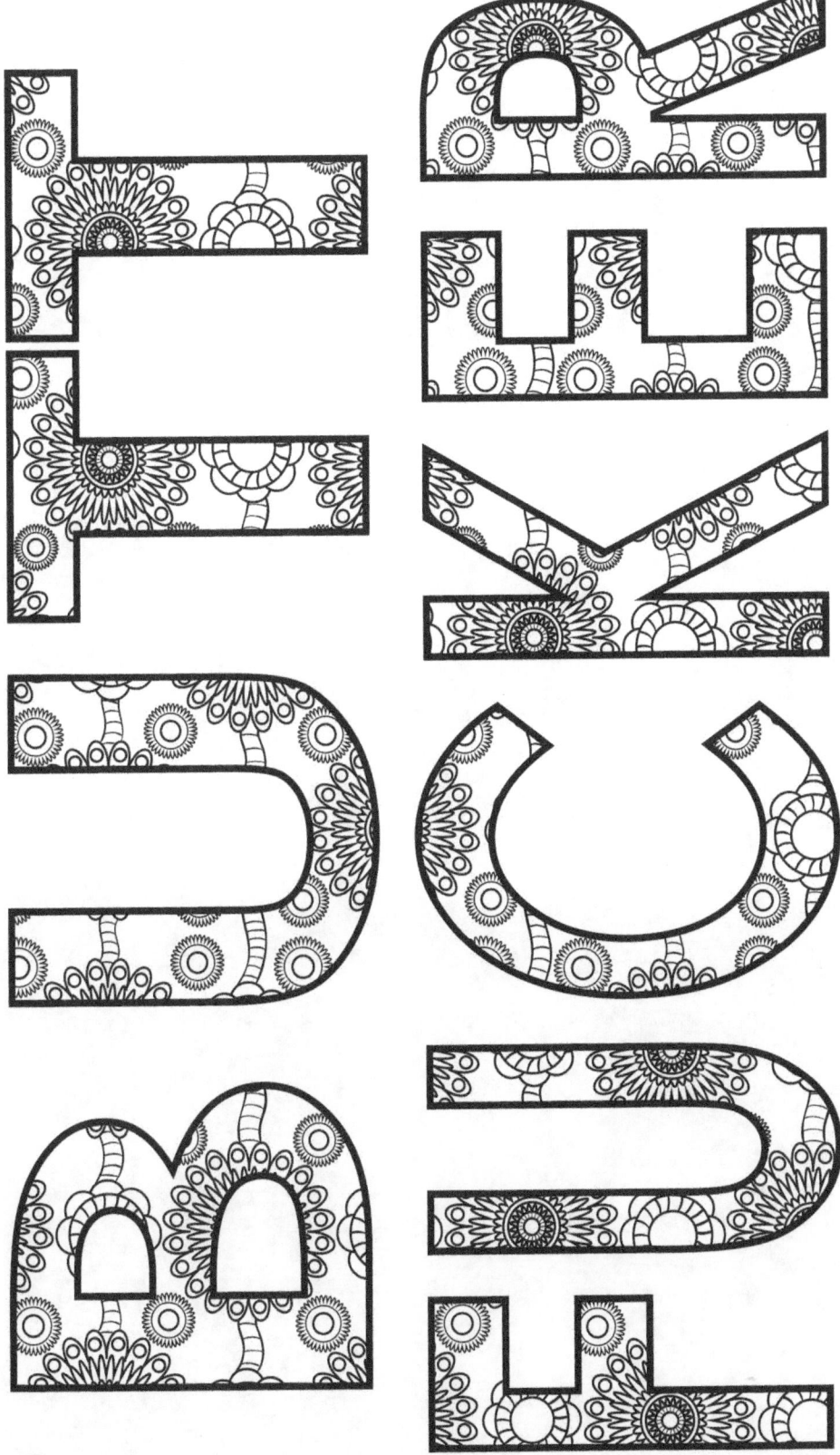

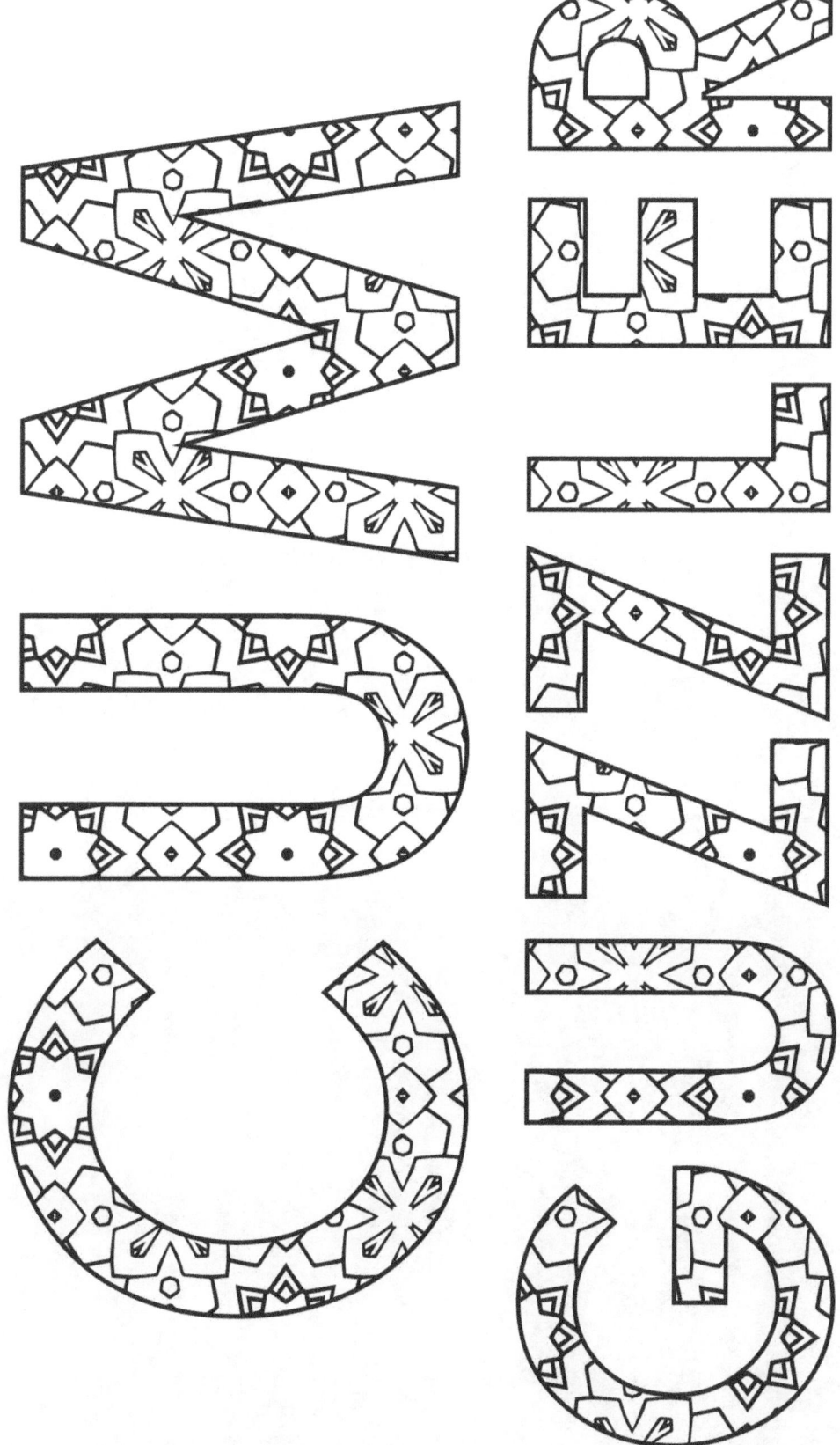

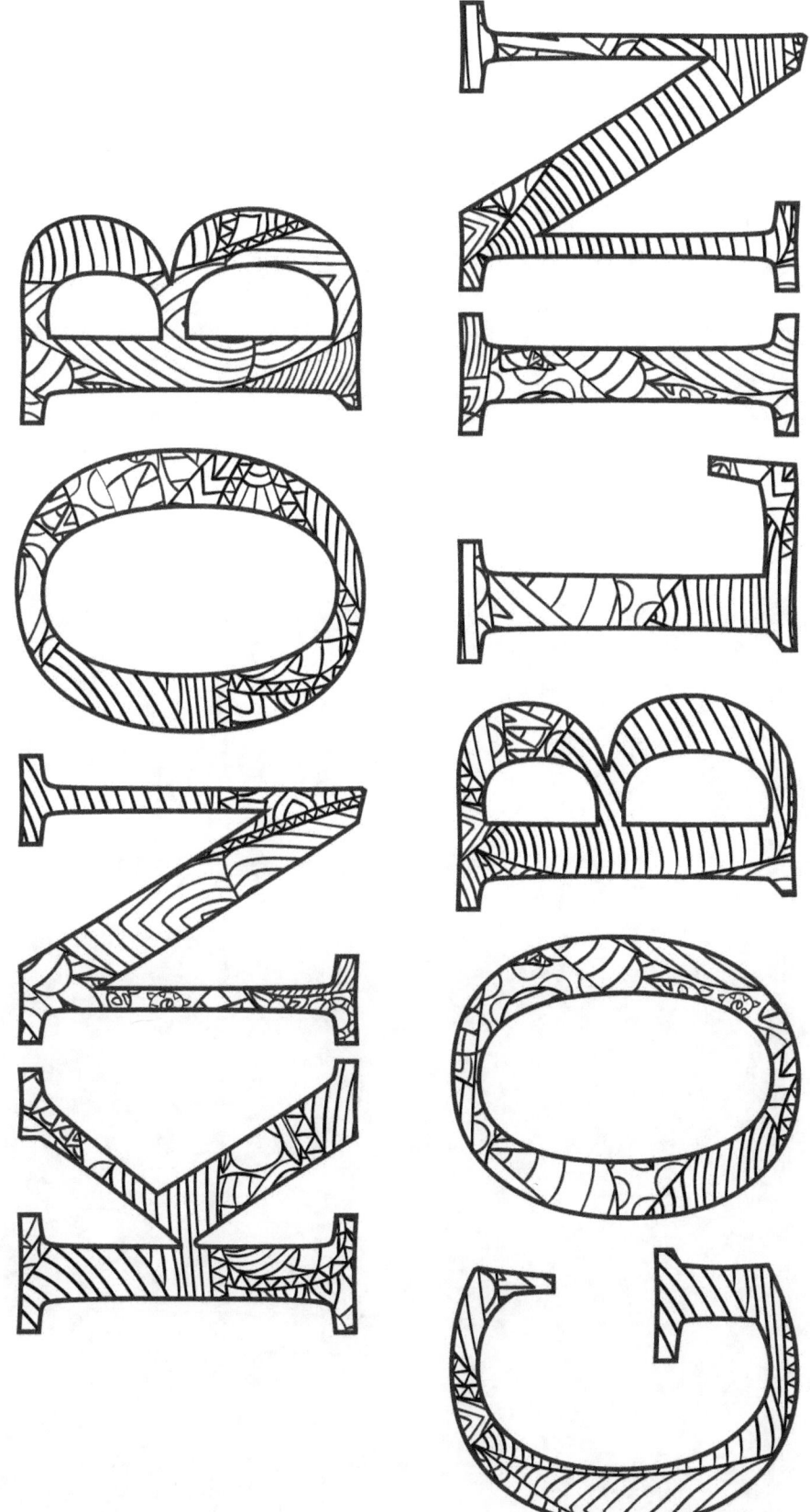

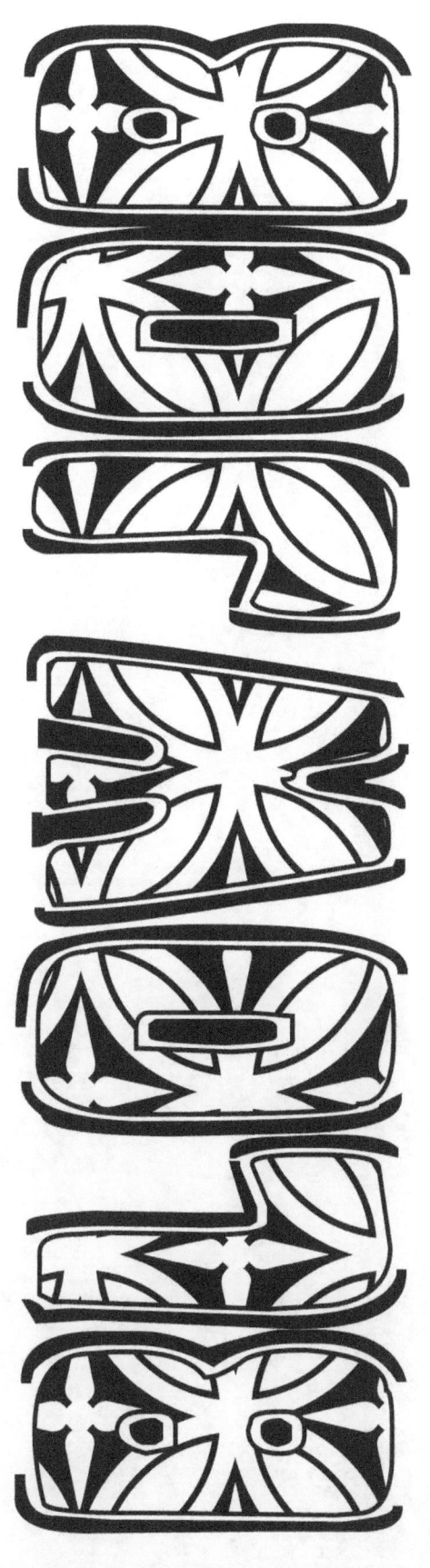

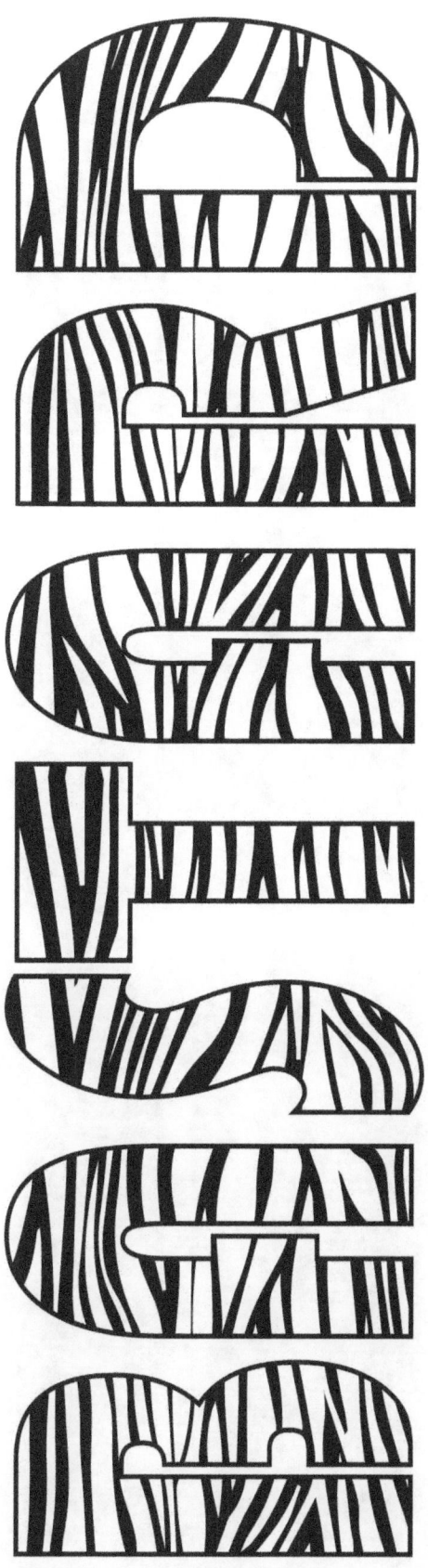

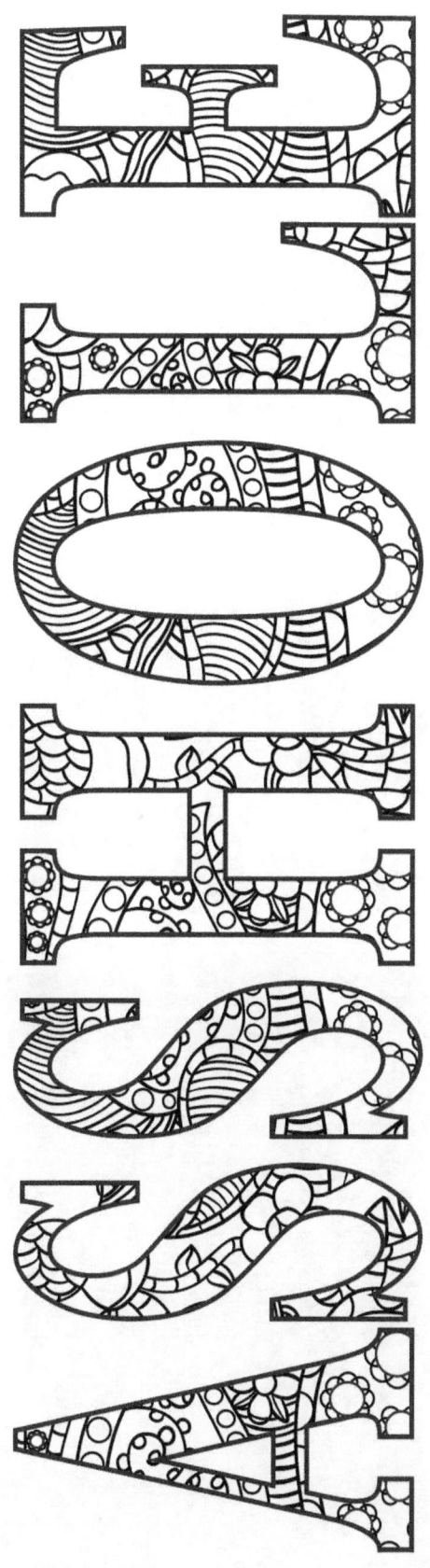

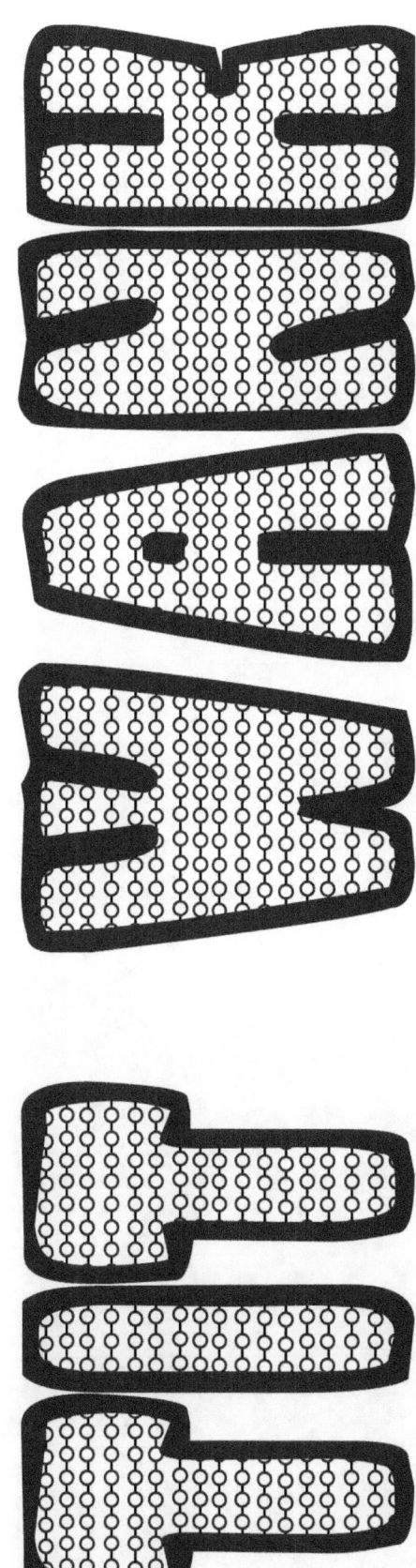

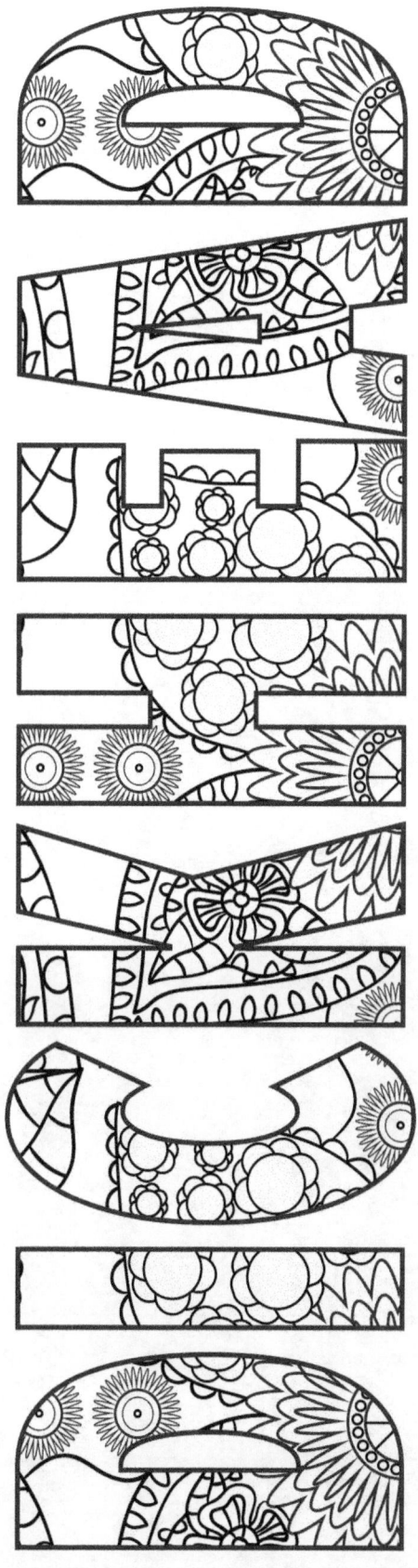

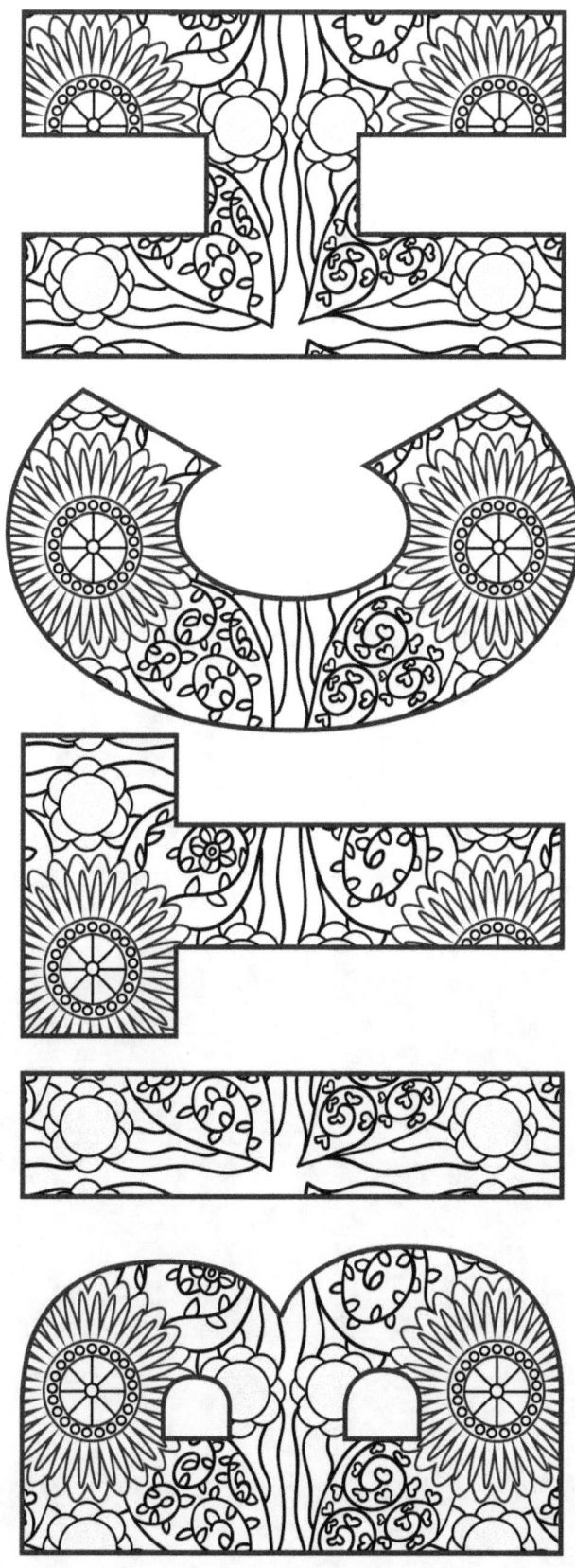

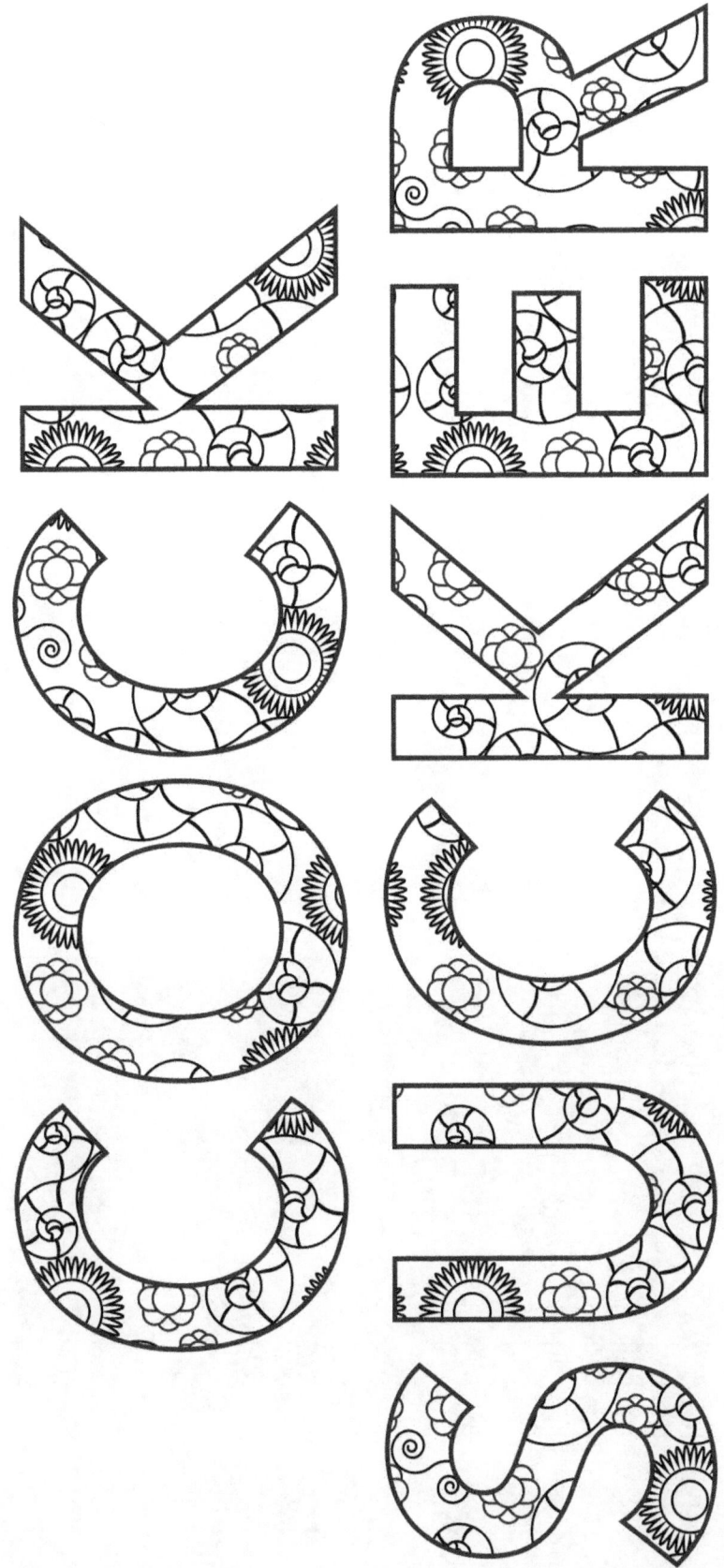

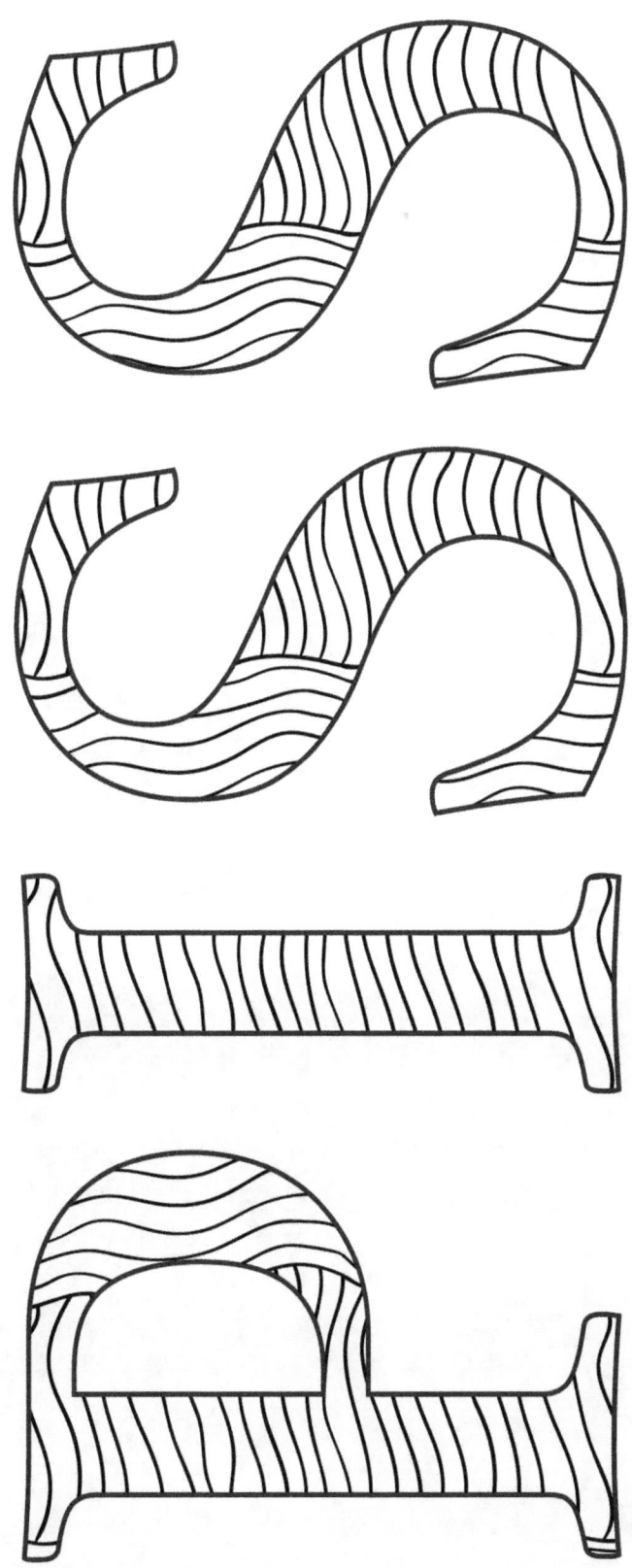

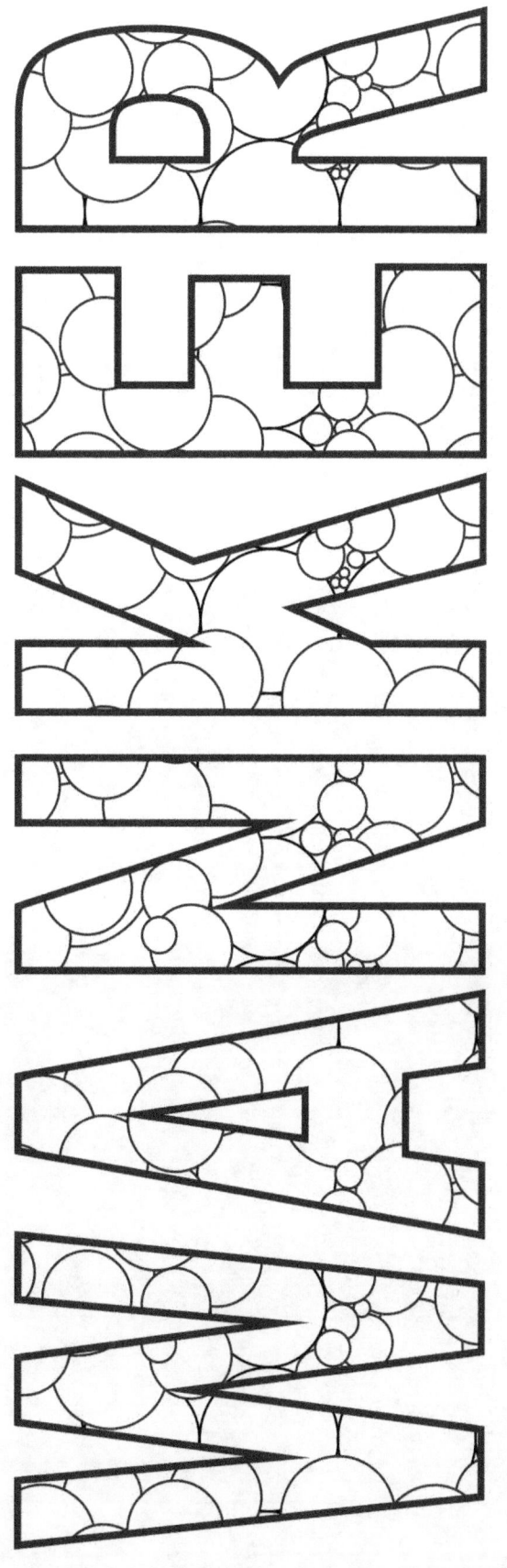

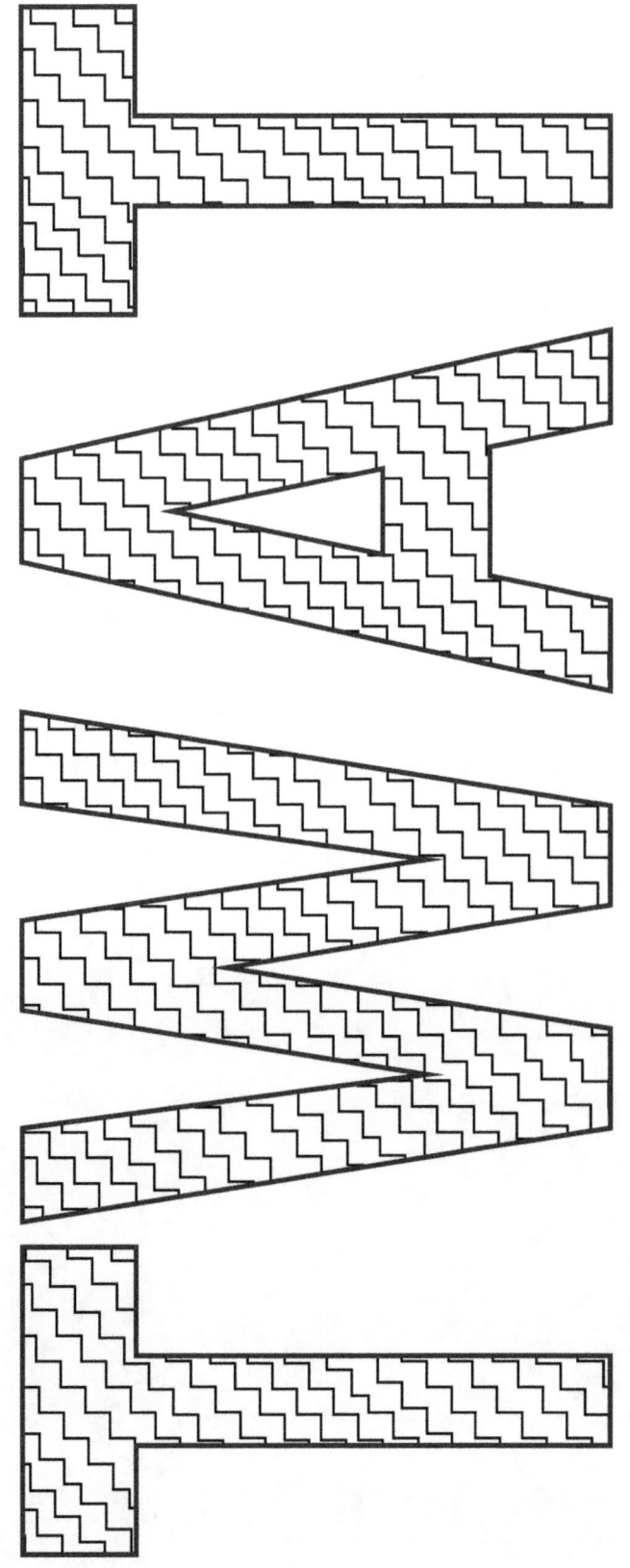

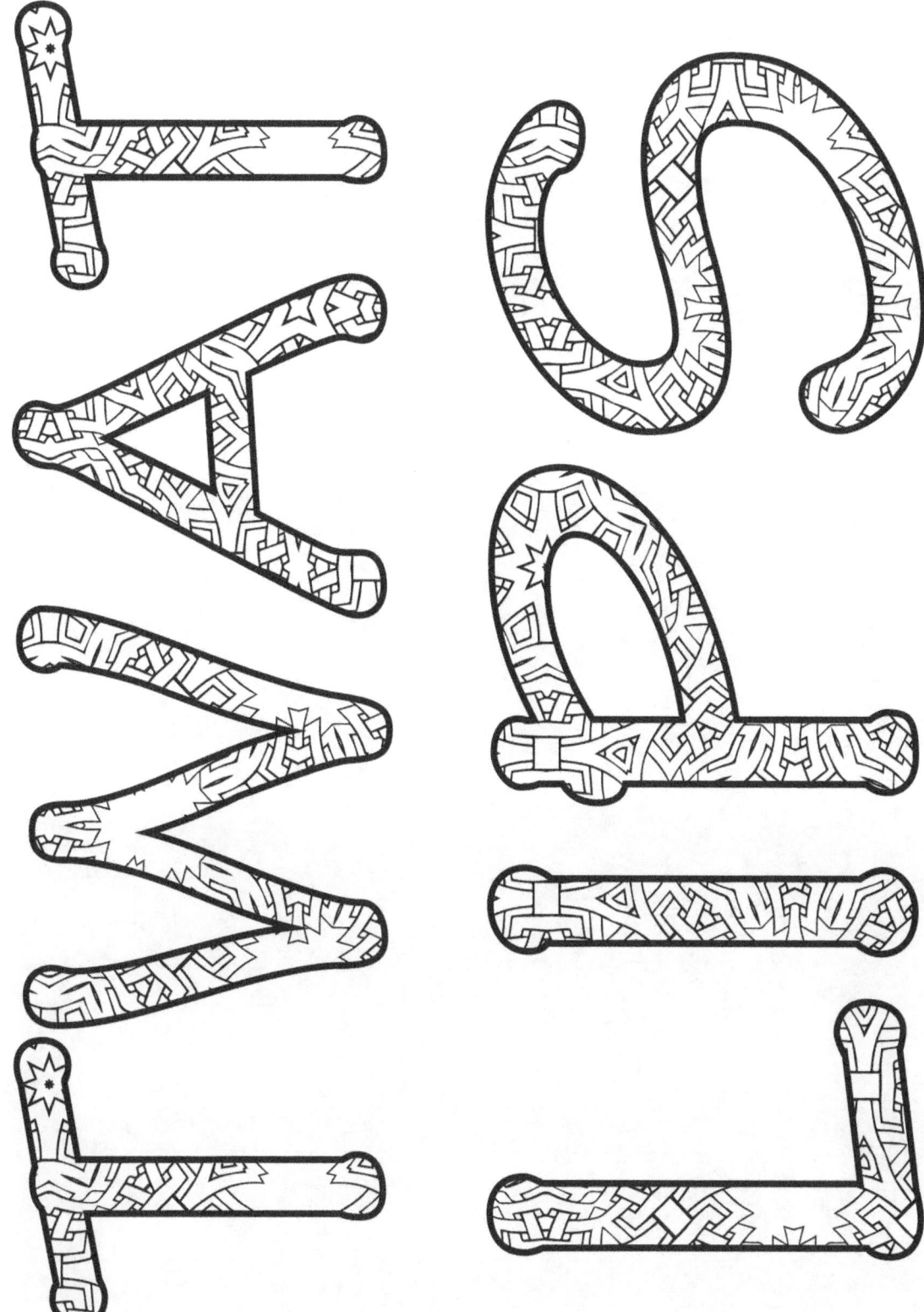

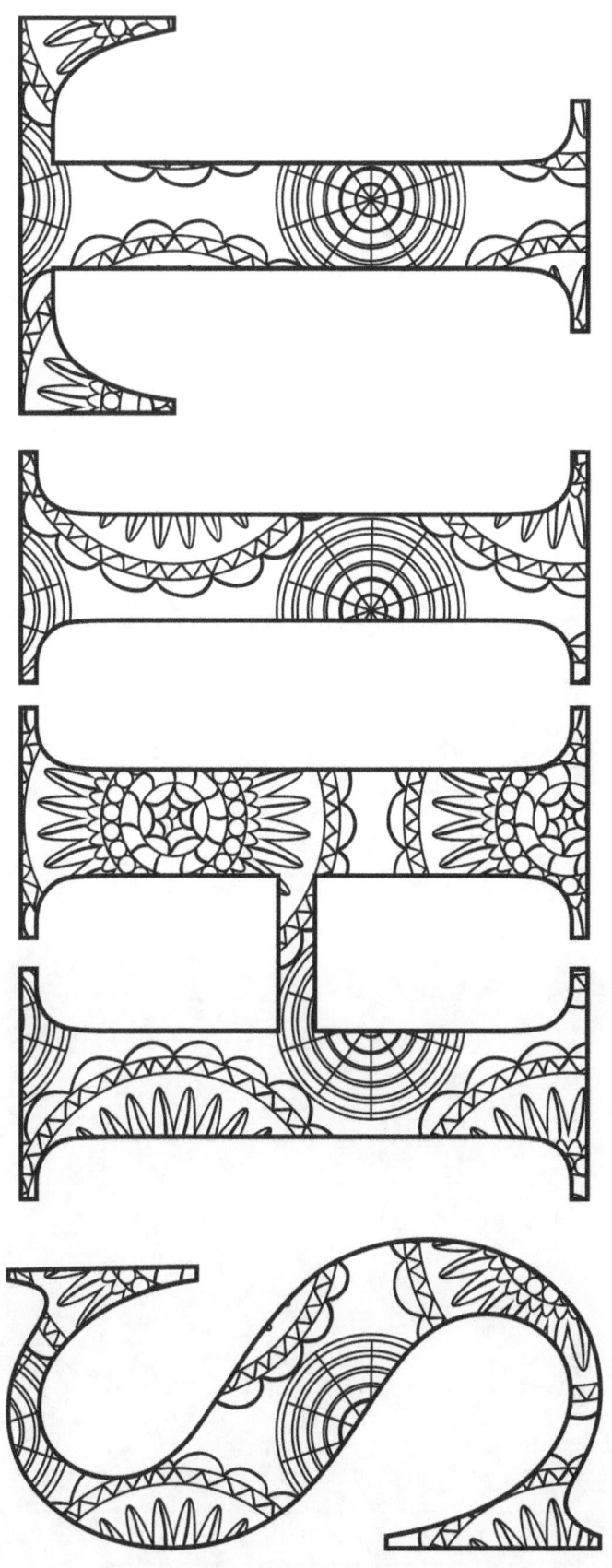

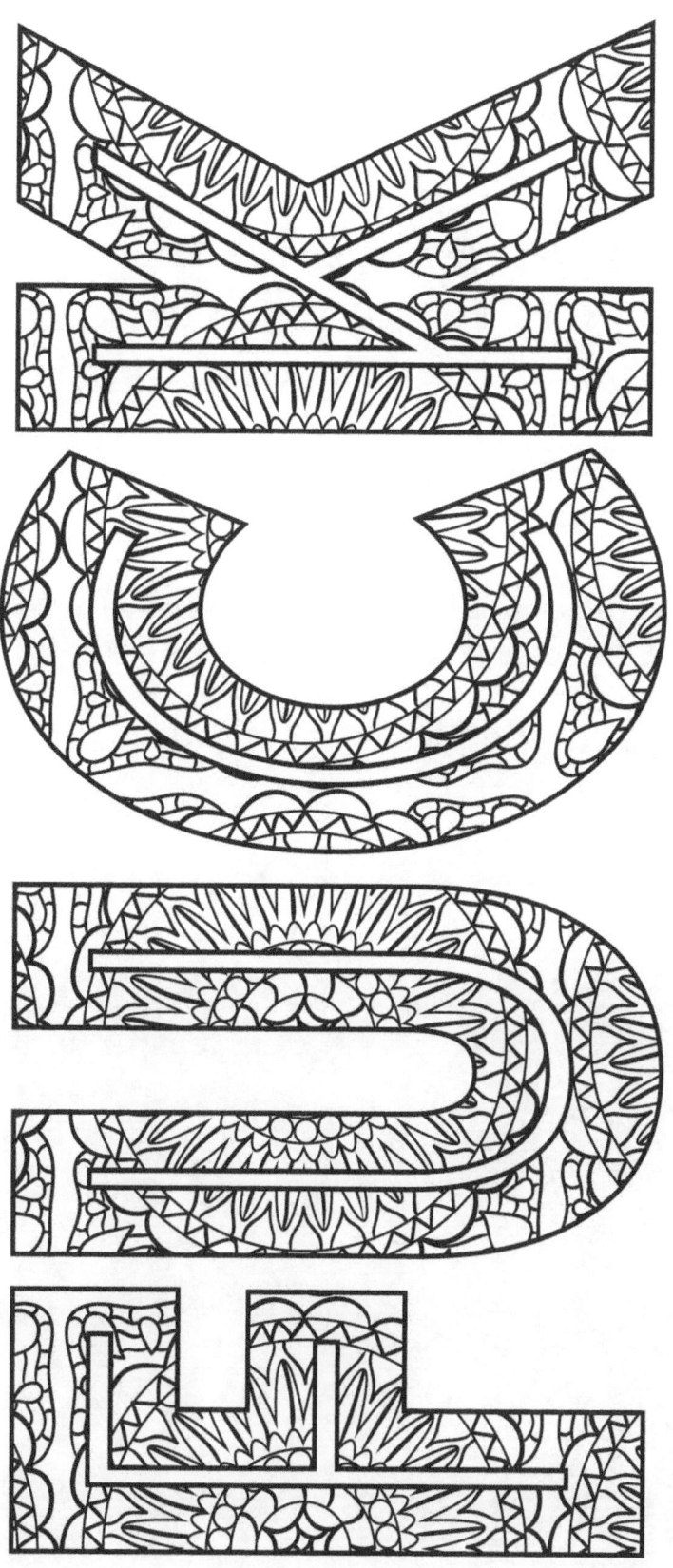

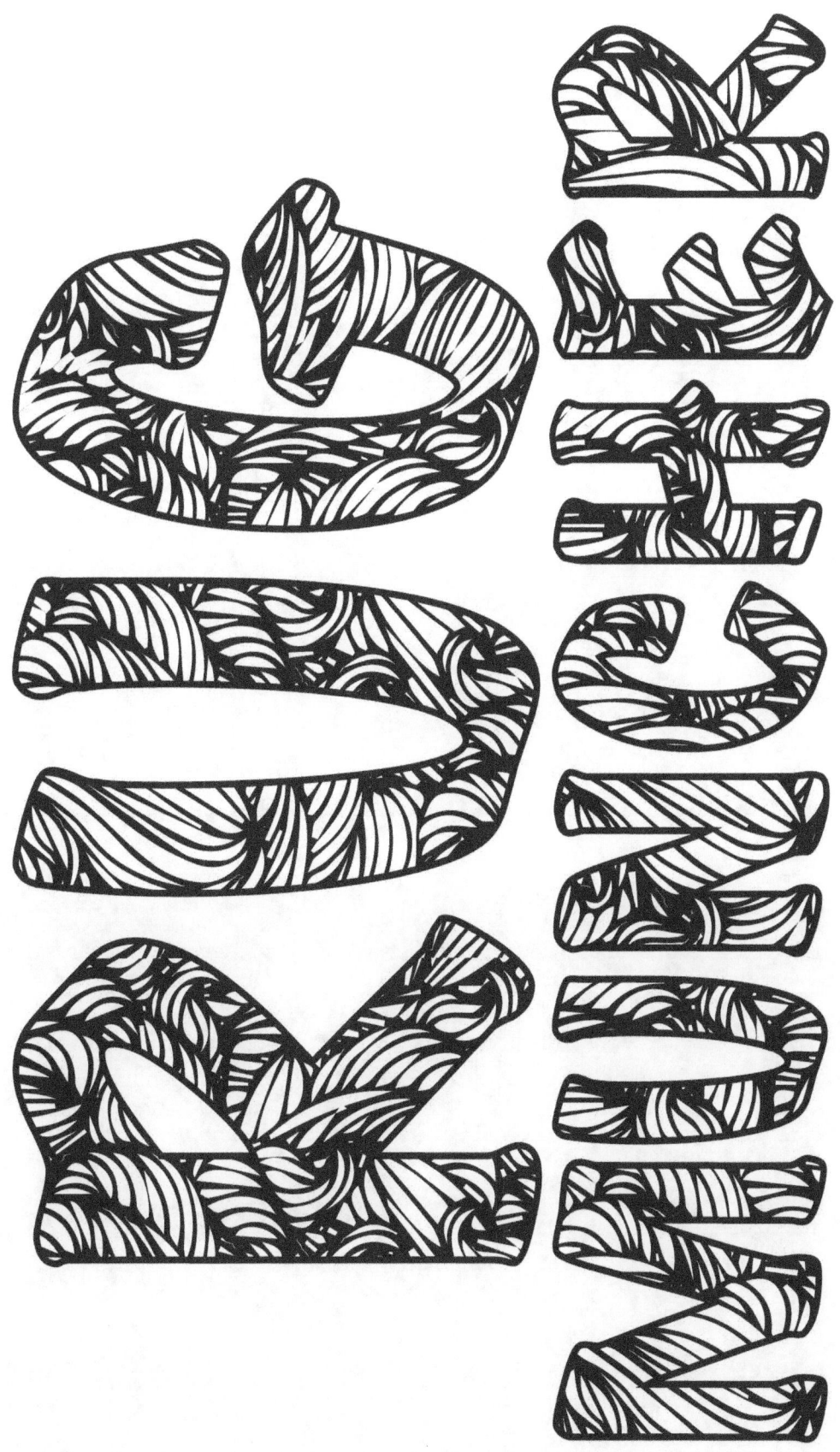

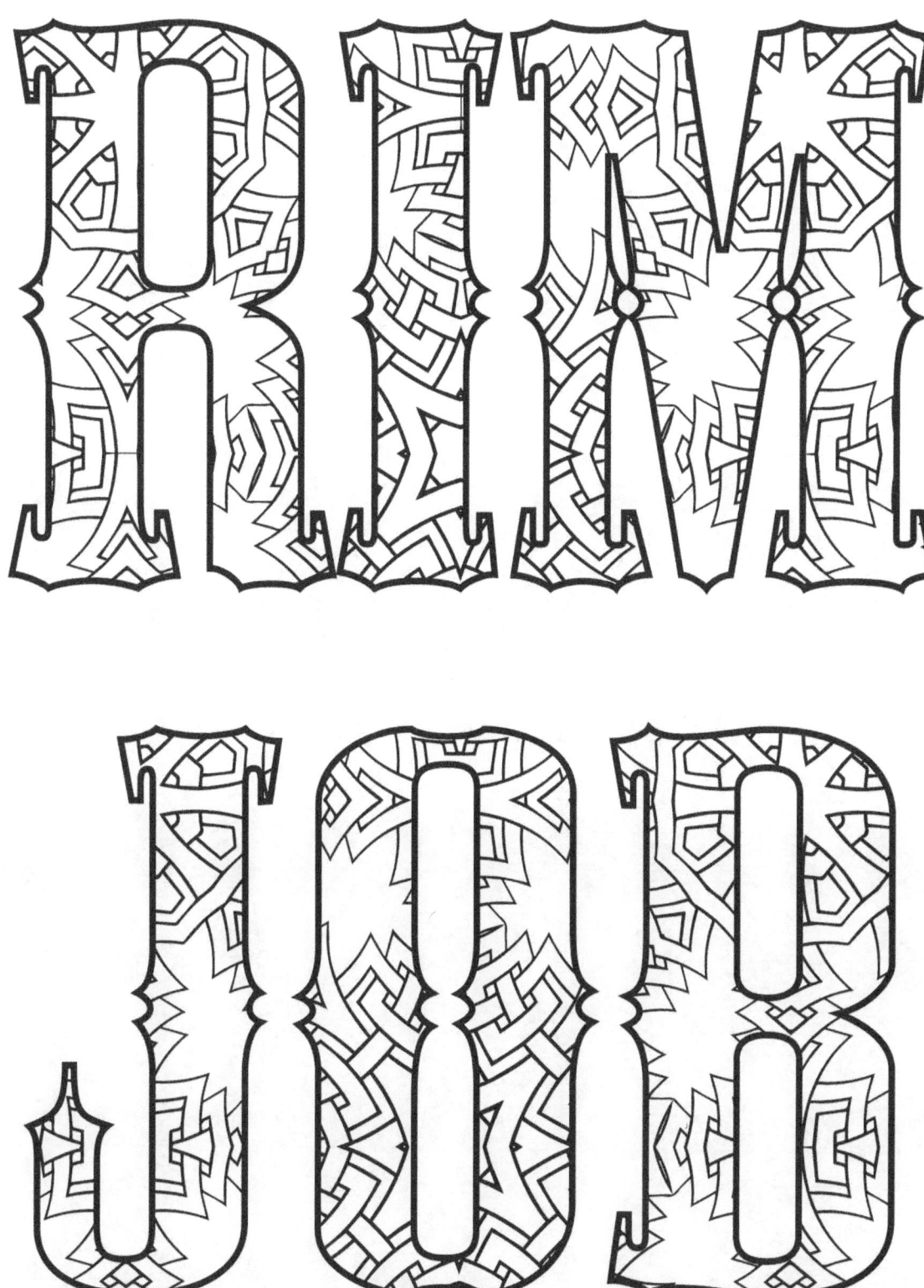

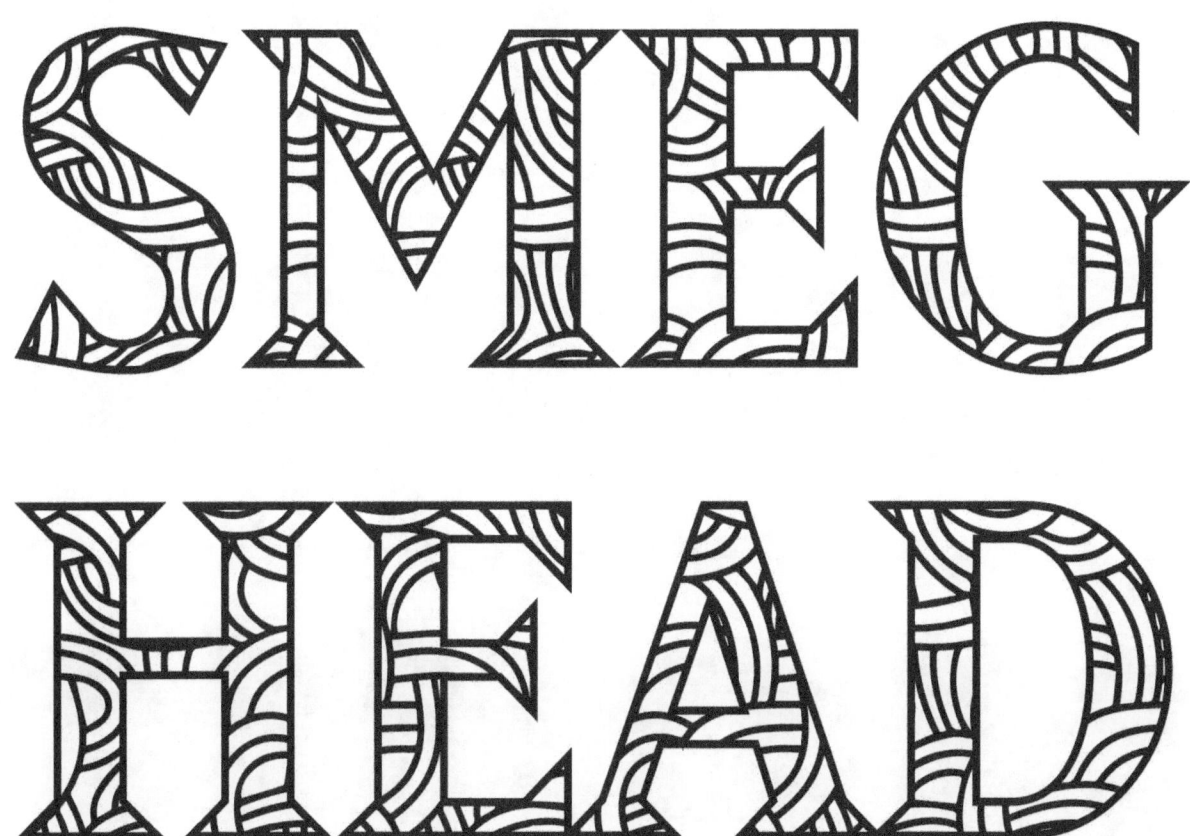

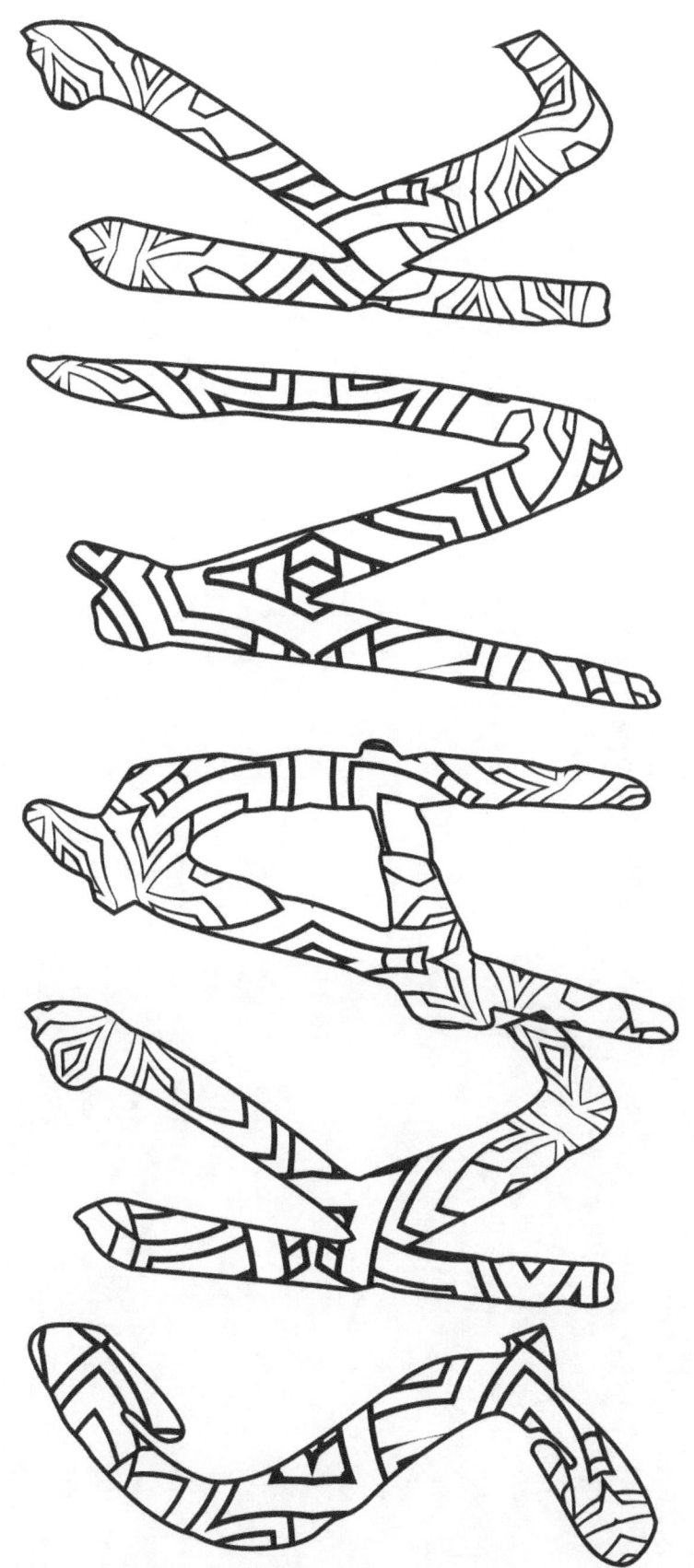

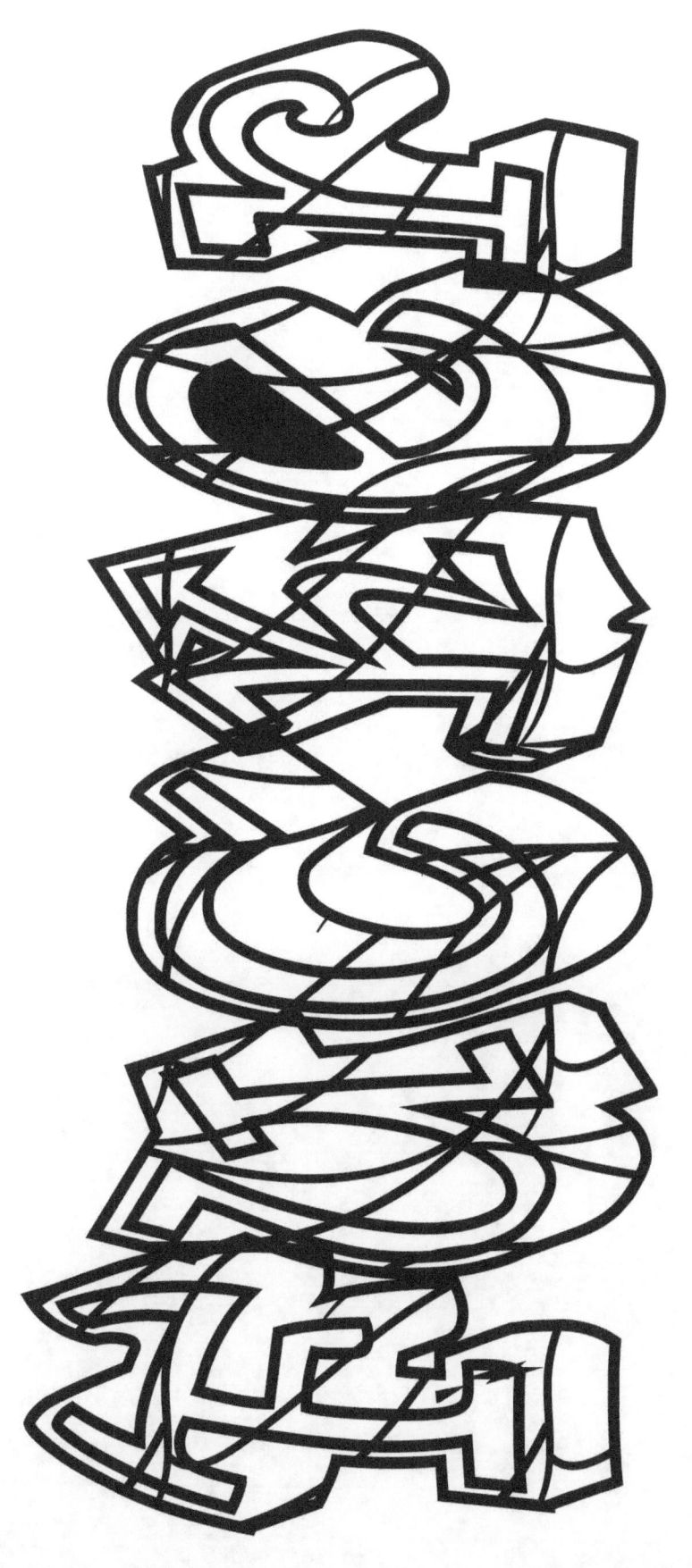

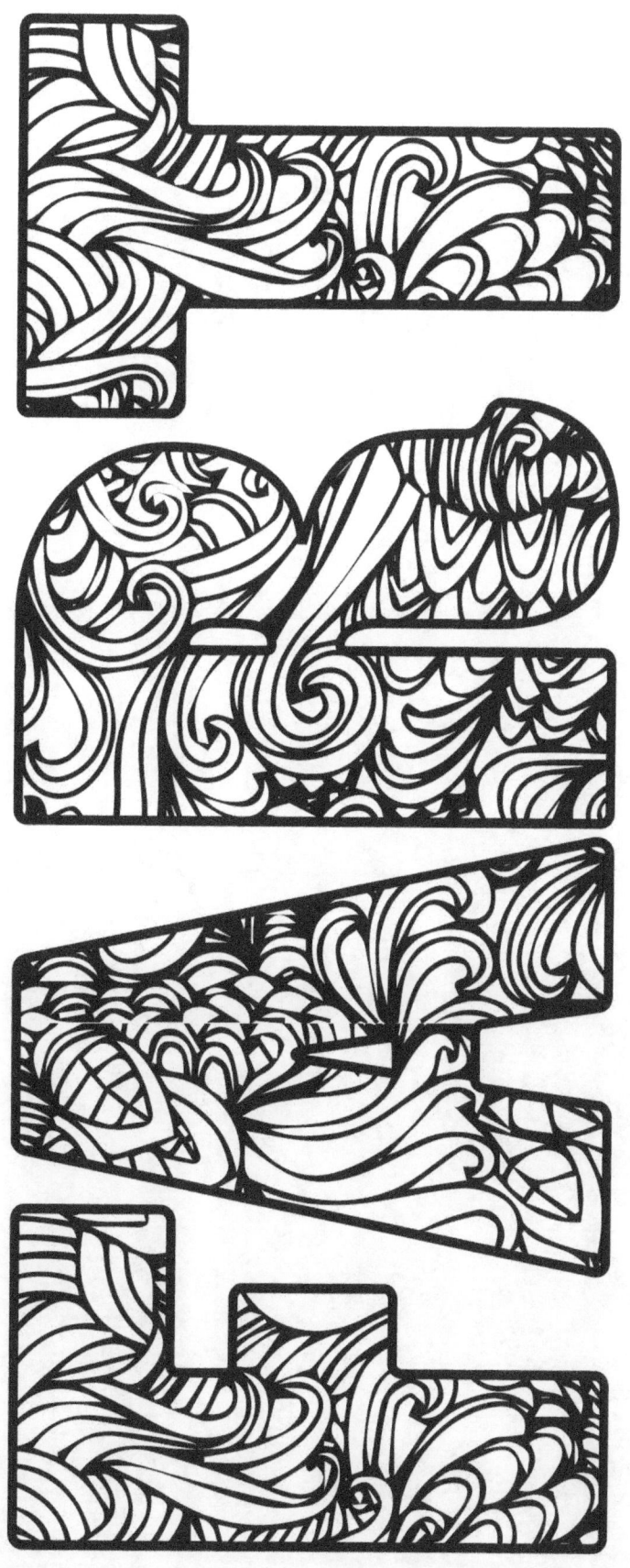

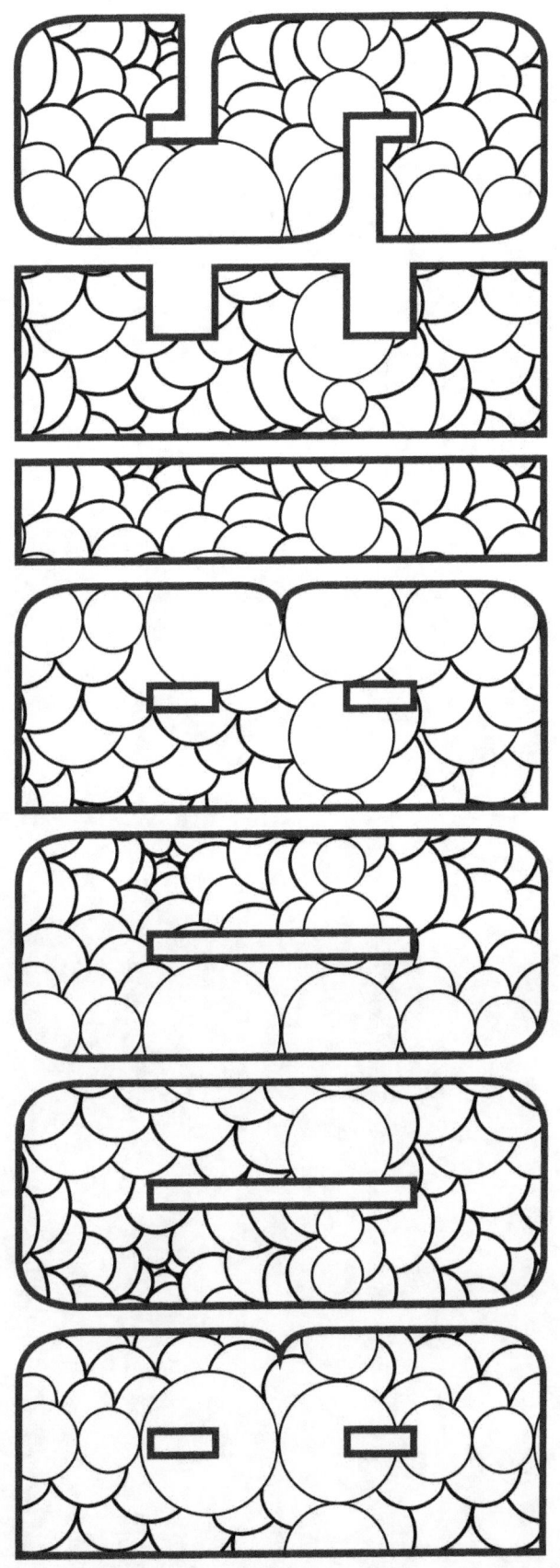

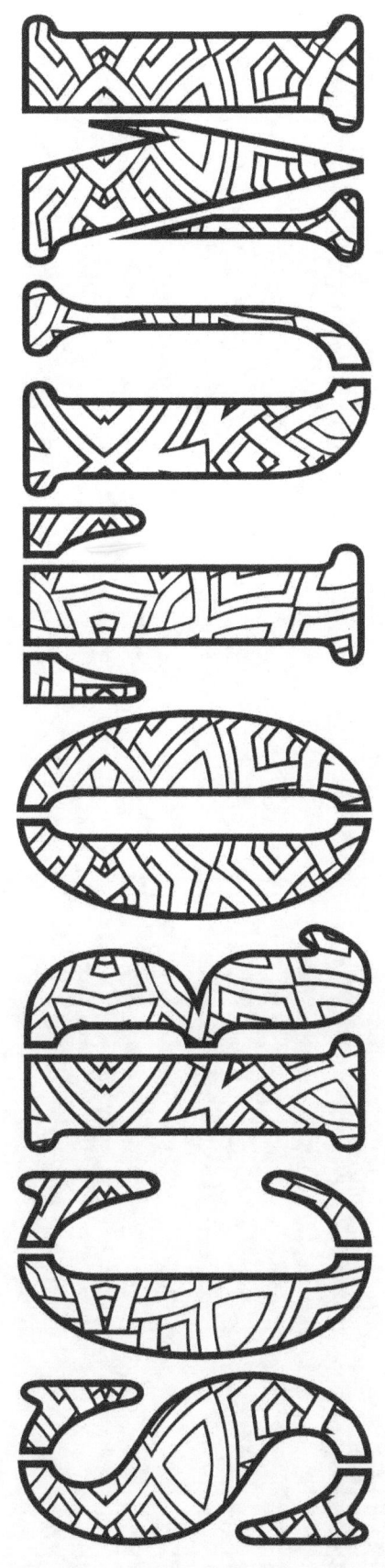

www.ingramcontent.com/pod-product-compliance
Lightning Source LLC
Chambersburg PA
CBHW080720190526
45169CB00006B/2444